Unit

# Polity Histories series

Kerry Brown, *China*
Emile Chabal, *France*
Alan Dowty, *Israel*
Jeff Kingston, *Japan*
David W. Lesch, *Syria*
Dmitri Trenin, *Russia*

# United Kingdom

**Adrian Bingham**

polity

Copyright © Adrian Bingham 2022

The right of Adrian Bingham to be identified as Author of this Work has been asserted in accordance with the UK Copyright, Designs and Patents Act 1988.

First published in 2022 by Polity Press

Polity Press
65 Bridge Street
Cambridge CB2 1UR, UK

Polity Press
111 River Street
Hoboken, NJ 07030, USA

All rights reserved. Except for the quotation of short passages for the purpose of criticism and review, no part of this publication may be reproduced, stored in a retrieval system or transmitted, in any form or by any means, electronic, mechanical, photocopying, recording or otherwise, without the prior permission of the publisher.

ISBN-13: 978-1-5095-3755-6
ISBN-13: 978-1-5095-3756-3 (pb)

A catalogue record for this book is available from the British Library.

Typeset in 11 on 13pt Berkeley
by Cheshire Typesetting Ltd, Cuddington, Cheshire
Printed and bound in the UK by TJ Books Limited

The publisher has used its best endeavours to ensure that the URLs for external websites referred to in this book are correct and active at the time of going to press. However, the publisher has no responsibility for the websites and can make no guarantee that a site will remain live or that the content is or will remain appropriate.

Every effort has been made to trace all copyright holders, but if any have been overlooked the publisher will be pleased to include any necessary credits in any subsequent reprint or edition.

For further information on Polity, visit our website:
politybooks.com

# Contents

*Map* vi
*Preface* vii

Introduction 1

1 Seeking a Role 17

2 The Pursuit of Economic Growth 49

3 From Cradle to Grave 80

4 A Disunited Kingdom? 108

5 People Power 138

6 Looking after Number 1 168

Afterword 198

*Further Reading* 201
*Notes* 205
*Index* 213

Map of the United Kingdom

# Preface

All historians are influenced by the times in which they write, especially so when those times are unusually dramatic. It would be foolish to pretend that this book has not been shaped by the political convulsions surrounding Brexit, and the unprecedented shutdowns forced by the Covid-19 pandemic. I have tried hard not to fall into the trap of writing a history that is defined by an inevitable contemporary endpoint, whether it be the departure from the European Union or the economic and welfare challenges posed by the new strains of coronavirus, but I'm sure that my analysis will have been informed and inflected by recent events. In one sense, though, my approach to this project is a very conscious response to what has been happening. One of the striking features of the extended public debates about Brexit and Covid-19 has been the prominence of simplistic and often inaccurate narratives about the United Kingdom's history – from celebrations of the global trading relationships that underpinned Victorian prosperity to invocations of the public spirit exemplified during our 'Finest Hour', the Second World War – and their use in suggesting lessons for the future. The populist historical-political discourse of recent years has reaffirmed my belief that we need more complex, multi-layered narratives about our recent past. There is no one story that we can tell that fully encapsulates the United Kingdom's post-Second World War history, not least because one central element of that history is the emergence of a more diverse, pluralistic, and mobile society. That is why I have chosen not to add to the pile of chronologically based histories, many of which are excellent. Comprehending our present situation, I would suggest, requires us to understand how different types of change – from broad shifts in global geopolitics and the structures of the world economy to social and cultural developments in localities and regions – have operated and intersected to shape everyday experiences and give individuals very different perspectives on the country they live in. It also involves explaining how the legacies of the UK's past have both shaped the present and, at times, complicated or obstructed attempts to create a better future. These two preoccupations – examining different layers of change, and addressing the tensions between past, present, and future – have determined the structure and content of this book.

A quick note on terminology. This book covers the United Kingdom of Great Britain and Northern Ireland, and I have consistently referred to the 'UK' and 'people of the UK' other than when I am specifically focusing upon the constituent nations of England, Scotland, Wales, or Northern Ireland. This can lead to some jarring notes when quoting others given that, in the early part of the period especially, it has been commonplace to refer to 'Britain' (or sometimes just 'England') when actually meaning the UK. There is also a risk of inelegant prose because the terminology of the UK does not offer an equivalent to 'Britons' to describe the citizens of the nation. Nevertheless, I have decided that accuracy and inclusivity favours use of the UK.

I would like to thank Louise Knight and Inès Boxman at Polity for their support when the writing of this book was repeatedly disrupted. My colleagues and students in the Department of History at the University of Sheffield have always provided me with a conducive environment for research and writing, Head of Department duties notwithstanding. Most of all, though, my love and thanks go to Felicity, Anna, and Thea: home has been a real haven while the pandemic has turned the world upside down.

# Introduction

In 1959, Hugh Thomas, a well-connected 28-year-old with literary ambitions, published a book called *The Establishment* despairing how the United Kingdom was dangerously stuck in the past. Nations which had achieved global success, he argued, became 'deeply and permanently marked' by their period of greatness. They invariably rested on their laurels and resisted innovation. The UK had followed this pattern, and its leaders – the 'Establishment' of the book's title – were now determined to defend the institutions of the glorious Victorian era with all their 'prejudices, ignorances and inhibitions'. Governments had been lured into 'supposing that, because Britain was once the greatest power, she must still aspire to the trappings, if not the facts, of continuing greatness'. This 'anachronistic frame of mind' spread into the cultural sphere so that people in other countries were 'far more intellectually and aesthetically alive' than those in the UK. Even the moral judgements of the previous century remained in place. Men were granted more freedom than women as long as they were discreet, but 'anything more blatant, more modern' was not permissible. 'To those who desire to see the resources and talents of Britain fully developed and extended,' he concluded with a flourish, 'there is no doubt that the fusty Establishment, with its Victorian views and standards of judgement, must be destroyed.'[1]

Thomas was no marginalized radical, jealous of the elites he railed against. The son of a British colonial officer based in what is now Ghana, he was educated at a top private boarding school, read History at the University of Cambridge, and then moved into a role at the Foreign Office. He resigned in 1957 in protest at the government's actions in the Middle East, but otherwise he was an insider in the very establishment he attacked. Thomas's polemic certainly resonated in some circles, and his was one of several books of the period agonizing over the 'state of the nation'. Yet it hardly captured the mood of the UK as a whole. The year *The Establishment* was published, 1959, also saw Prime Minister Harold Macmillan lead the governing Conservative Party to its third consecutive election victory, successfully appealing to voters not to endanger the unprecedented prosperity that was visible across the UK. Two years earlier, Macmillan had famously remarked that 'most of our people have never had it so good', and his party's election slogan in 1959 was 'Life's Better with the Conservatives, Don't Let Labour Ruin It'. The claim that 'life's better' seemed eminently plausible. With rising real wages, very little unemployment, and a housing boom that allowed many to move into more comfortable surroundings, it was easy to believe that a more modern and affluent UK had arrived.

There were plenty of signs of the future for those able to spot them. The first section of the M1 motorway opened in November 1959, catering to the 30% of households that now owned cars. Some travelled in the recently released Mini, a small two-door car that would become an icon of forward-looking British design. The same year, Barclays became the first bank to use an electronic computer. In a nod to the emerging power of youth culture, the British Broadcasting Corporation (BBC) launched the television programme *Jukebox Jury* to assess new popular music records. In St Pancras Town Hall, London, meanwhile, the Trinidadian writer and activist Claudia Jones organized a 'Caribbean Carnival' to showcase the vibrancy of the culture of the many people who had travelled to the UK from the West Indies. This event would become the forerunner of the long-lasting Notting Hill Carnival. When viewed from this perspective, the UK did not look like a nation stuck in the Victorian era, or resting on its laurels. Thomas was no more than half right. The UK was indeed uniquely shaped by legacies of past greatness, but these were not strong enough entirely to constrain the powerful forces of change that were creating a very different society. The result was a nation of many contrasts, with pageantry and tradition co-existing alongside innovation and a yearning for the modern.

This book tells the history of the UK since 1945 by exploring these tensions between the past, present, and future. At one level, the UK has had no reason to be anxious about the future. By almost any measure, it remains one of the world's leading nations. It is one of the five permanent members of the United Nations Security Council, and a founder member of the North Atlantic Treaty Organization (NATO), the International Monetary Fund (IMF), and the World Bank. In 1952, it became the third country with nuclear weapons, after the United States and the Soviet Union. Its economy has stayed within the top six in the world by size, and the City of London is a leading financial centre. The UK's (former) empire ensures that it has connections and interests around the globe, and it is the home of the world's predominant language, English. The stability of its political system, and its respect for individual rights, are widely admired. It boasts some of the world's most prestigious universities and a highly advanced science and technology sector. Its popular culture – the Beatles and the Rolling Stones, James Bond and Harry Potter – is consumed far and wide, and its football clubs have larger fanbases than any others.

But these very real strengths do not necessarily live up to the expectations created by the past, and, as a consequence, the UK since 1945 has been haunted by a sense of decline. In the nineteenth century, the UK had emerged as the first industrial nation and the world's greatest power, the centre of an empire more extensive than any previously seen. This global success cast a hallowed glow over its institutions, particularly its parliamentary and constitutional structures, many of which dated back hundreds of years. In a time of racialized thinking, many regarded military victories and economic prosperity as a reflection of the superiority of UK citizens, especially in relation to colonized populations. Others believed that the UK's Protestant virtue ensured it was favoured by divine grace. Even if the strategic and economic environments became much more competitive in the twentieth century, victories in the First and Second World Wars reinforced the narrative of the UK's exceptionalism and further legitimized its democracy. Winston Churchill, the UK's prime minister between 1940 and 1945, was steeped in evocative tales of the nation's heroic past, and presented the exploits of wartime as the next episode – indeed, the 'Finest Hour' – of a glorious history.

After 1945, and certainly after 1956, it was very difficult to maintain the celebratory rhetoric. The United States and the Soviet Union emerged as unrivalled superpowers as the UK struggled to support its imperial commitments. As we will see in Chapter 1, the failed intervention in response to Egypt's nationalization of the Suez Canal in 1956 exposed the UK's inability to act as an independent great power without the blessing of the United States. Even if Macmillan could plausibly tell voters that 'life's better', Thomas's concerns about economic stagnation were by no means unfounded by the late 1950s. The UK's productivity and growth rates lagged behind its main competitors, and the industries that had underpinned

Victorian prosperity were on a downwards trajectory. At the same time, the significant expansion of the West Indian and Asian communities in the UK ensured that older nations of racial superiority were fiercely challenged. By the early 1970s, most of the former empire had secured independence, and the UK was routinely being described as the 'sick man of Europe'. Much political debate was focused on how to recover former glories, and what elements of the past needed to be taken forward into the future. Many solutions were proposed, from joining the European Community to reforming the state and reshaping the UK economy. It is interesting to note that by the 1980s, Hugh Thomas, now an acclaimed historian, had come to see a reforming Conservative prime minister, Margaret Thatcher, as the best means of reviving the UK's fortunes. His personal reward was to be ennobled as Lord Thomas of Swynnerton, and indisputably become a member of the establishment he had once sought to destroy. Individual stories, and aspirations, were intimately intertwined with these wider debates. This was certainly the case thirty years later, when Boris Johnson, another expensively educated writer and politician, rose to the premiership by channelling Churchill and Thatcher and offering Brexit as the means of providing the UK with a better future.

All nations, of course, are shaped by the tensions between past and present, but these pressures were unusually intense in the UK because of the country's period of unprecedented global power, and the speed with which this power unravelled in the years after 1945. An empire accumulated over centuries was virtually gone within twenty-five years. Industries that had powered the economy for over a century declined precipitously. Equally important was the strong sense of continuity that governed political life in the UK. Unlike almost all European nations, the UK did not experience a decisive moment of rupture in the modern period: there were no revolutions, no moments of constitution-making, no invasions or significant military defeats to usher in a new regime, conspicuously alter political dynamics, or dramatically change the balance of social forces. The UK experienced its civil war in the mid-seventeenth century, and the 'Glorious Revolution' of 1688–9 confirmed the primacy of parliament over the monarchy. After that, its political system developed incrementally and relatively peacefully. The important exception here was Ireland, which did witness political violence, civil war, and partition, but this was routinely marginalized from accounts of national history, and indeed was a central reason for the focus on Britain rather than the United Kingdom as the imagined community. It could be conveniently explained that the Protestant mainland was not beset by the same sectarian tensions and social problems that Catholicism had supposedly generated across the Irish Sea.

In the absence of these moments of rupture, many of the institutions, practices, and symbols of the past remained conspicuous – most obviously in the form of the monarchy, royal household, and privy council, but also in the rituals of parliament and court room, in the traditions of the first-past-the-post electoral system, in the secrecy that cloaked many of the operations of the central state and the military. For the champions of this history, it was precisely the wisdom accumulated in this stable political system that explained the UK's successes; the adaptability, moderation, and pragmatism of its governing structures prevented the crises and extremism that beset many of its European neighbours. As the UK's circumstances changed after 1945, though, critics like Thomas could point to these legacies as signs of backwardness and a failure to come to terms with modernity. For these observers, the UK needed a codified constitution, a proper separation of powers, a more representative parliamentary system, and an end to the fawning over an outdated monarchy. The battle between past and future ran through the heart of UK politics.

## *The UK: A Brief History*

Before turning to the years after 1945, it is worth saying a little more about the UK's longer history. The UK itself was formed in 1800, and is by no means as old as many of the institutions which it now incorporates. The coming together of England, Wales, Scotland, and Ireland into one political unit was not an inevitability, but rather the result of an interplay of political, economic, and military factors over several centuries. The expansionist ambitions of the English monarchy were evident in the twelfth and thirteenth centuries through significant incursions into Ireland and Wales, although Scotland managed to retain its independence. By the mid-sixteenth century, Wales was incorporated into the English state and run from London, while Ireland was forced to accept Henry VIII as king and was subjected to attempts at colonization. England and Scotland were joined dynastically when James I (of England) and VI (of Scotland) came to the throne in 1603, and this became a political union in 1707 when England and Wales signed the Act of Union with Scotland to form the Kingdom of Great Britain. The separate Scottish parliament was prorogued, and Scottish MPs sat in a united parliament in the Palace of Westminster in London, although distinctive religious and legal structures remained. While England, Wales, and Scotland became Protestant during the Reformation of the sixteenth and seventeenth centuries, the bulk of the Irish population remained Catholic, setting up an ongoing tension with Protestant colonizers from the British mainland. The ambitious British state could not countenance the strategic uncertainty posed by this difficult situation and in 1800 imposed an Act of Union with Ireland. On 1 January 1801, the United Kingdom of Great Britain and Ireland came into being, and 100 MPs from Ireland took their seats at Westminster.

By 1801, the United Kingdom was already a global power. Explorers and adventurers from England travelled to North America, the Caribbean, Africa, and Asia from the late sixteenth century in search of glory and gold. The first lasting overseas settlement was established in Jamestown (in the modern US state of Virginia) in 1607, and over the coming decades further colonies were established in North America, Bermuda, Barbados, and Jamaica. Jamaica would become a hub of the lucrative slave trade, which Britain dominated in the eighteenth century, until ending the practice in 1807. Manufactured products were taken from Britain to West Africa to be sold for slaves, who were then transported, in appalling conditions, to the plantations of the West Indies and North America; sugar, molasses, and other goods returned to British ports such as Bristol and Liverpool. It is estimated that Britain transported around 3.1 million Africans; some 400,000 did not even survive the journey.[2] From the mid-seventeenth century, English trading posts were also established on the Indian subcontinent under the umbrella of the East India Company, and by the second half of the eighteenth century this was becoming a substantial territorial empire. In the 1770s and 1780s, Britain made claims on New Zealand and Australia. This expansion was always contested, both by local rulers and by rival European empires, and there were defeats along the way, most notably in North America when the thirteen colonies successfully asserted their independence as the United States and, with French support, defeated the British military operation (although Canadian territories were retained). But the underlying strength of its economy, and the associated power of its unmatched navy, ensured that Britain was hard to contain. Between 1793 and 1815, Britain/the UK waged a global war against France, its main imperial rival, and eventually won a decisive victory, establishing maritime dominance for the next 100 years. Over the course of the nineteenth century, the UK consolidated its position in India, South Africa, Australia, the Caribbean, and Canada, extended its claims into Singapore, Hong Kong, Cyprus, and new parts of Southern and Eastern Africa, and used its military and economic muscle to open up trade with countries that were not part of the formal empire, notably in South America and China. The empire would reach its fullest extent immediately after the First World War, when the UK acquired the West and East African colonies previously held by Germany, as well as being given League of Nations mandates for Iraq, Transjordan, and Palestine. In 1920, 413 million people, nearly a quarter of the world's population, lived under the UK flag.

These global connections, the resources that were extracted from them, and the market opportunities that they delivered helped to sustain, and were in turn sustained by, the rapid industrialization of the UK from the late eighteenth century. The UK economy was transformed by the introduction of machine power to supplement human or animal labour, the emergence of more specialized and standardized workplace roles, and the concentration of labour in factories which could benefit from economies of scale. The technological innovations of the spinning mule, the power loom, and the steam engine enabled cotton goods to be produced with far greater efficiency, and Manchester and the surrounding area became the global hub of the textile industry. Steam power also revolutionized coal production and iron manufacture, often found in the same areas, including Tyneside, South Yorkshire, South Wales, and central Scotland. The UK raced into a significant lead over its economic competitors: by the middle of the nineteenth century, it produced around half of the world's cotton and pig iron, and some two-thirds of the world's coal. In the second half of the century, the UK achieved similar success in the fields of steel production and ship-building: by 1911, it constructed about 70% of the world's sea-going ships. Coal production continued to rise, peaking in 1913, by which point around a million people worked in mining. Industrialization was underpinned by rapid population growth and urbanization, and it altered the internal dynamics of the UK: cities such as Glasgow, Swansea, Cardiff, Manchester, Sheffield, and Newcastle all emerged as densely populated industrial powerhouses, and the ever-expanding railway network ensured faster connections between them.

In many respects, the First World War marked the end of the UK's period of global dominance, despite it emerging victorious from four years of bloody mechanized conflict. As well as causing the loss of nearly three-quarters of a million UK citizens, the war effort put an immense strain on the nation's finances and disrupted its global trading patterns. The industries that had powered Victorian prosperity were now experiencing fierce competition, and in the 1920s and 1930s there was mass unemployment in regions dependent on coal mining, textiles, iron and steel, and shipbuilding. The war also exacerbated the worsening tensions in Ireland. The nationalist Easter Rising in Dublin in 1916 was brutally suppressed by British troops, but sweeping victories for the nationalist Sinn Féin party once the war ended created an unstable situation that was only resolved by partition. The 1920 Government of Ireland Act, and the subsequent Anglo-Irish Treaty of 1921, created Northern Ireland from the six, predominantly Protestant, north-eastern counties (Antrim, Armagh, Down, Fermanagh, Londonderry, and Tyrone), while the other twenty-six counties formed the Irish Free State as an independent dominion within the British Empire. (In 1949, this would become the entirely independent Republic of Ireland.) The UK henceforth became the United Kingdom of Great Britain and Northern Ireland.

Despite these pressures, the UK successfully managed the transition to a full democracy, and did not fall prey to the political extremism that marked most European nations in the inter-war period. After gradual extensions of the franchise over the nineteenth century, in 1918 all men, and most women over 30, were given the vote. Ten years later, women won the vote on the same terms as men, at the age of 21. The Labour Party emerged to champion the interests of trade unions and working people, but the Conservative Party, alone or in coalition, was the dominant political force in the two decades after 1918. The UK's long-standing and flexible constitutional arrangements survived the Irish crisis and the economic depression of the 1930s, and a Conservative-dominated National Government, led by Prime Minister Neville Chamberlain, reluctantly took the nation to war with Germany in September 1939 to counter the expansionism of Hitler's Nazi regime.

The UK's experience in the Second World War was very different from that in the First. Rather than extended attritional warfare in the trenches, the focus for UK efforts between 1940 and 1944 was in the air and at sea, and military losses were about half of those suffered in the previous conflict. This time, however, sustained German bombing brought the UK mainland into the front line, with significant civilian losses and urban destruction during the 'Blitz' of 1940–1. Criticisms of the UK war effort led to Winston Churchill becoming prime minister in May 1940, and he sustained UK morale while an alliance was built with the United States and the Soviet Union that was capable of defeating Germany, Italy, and Japan. The victory that was celebrated in May 1945 seemed to vindicate once again the UK's institutions and democracy – this had been framed very much as a 'People's War' – but it would become clear over subsequent years that it would be increasingly difficult for the nation to sustain the global role that it had enjoyed for over a century.

## Writing the History of the UK

How should we tell the complex history of the UK after 1945? The obvious answer is to construct a chronological narrative, and there are many fine works that adopt this approach. While this can lead to a compelling and comprehensible story, however, there are several downsides too, especially in a shorter book such as this. Chronological national histories tend to focus attention on the actions of political leaders and central government, and to identify general elections as key turning points; it is far harder to integrate changes driven by longer-term economic, social, cultural, and technological developments, or to bring out the experiences of ordinary people. This is a particular problem, I would argue, when one of the main features of the UK since 1945 is the emergence of a more pluralistic and diverse society in which different individuals have had very different experiences. UK politics and culture are already saturated with simplistic popular historical narratives, and there is much to be gained by writing the national story in a less familiar and potentially more challenging way.

This book is therefore structured thematically, and will examine in turn six layers of the UK experience, moving scale from the macro (UK in the world) to the micro (the individual within the UK). This will allow the book to explore, and integrate, different processes of change, and consider how power is exercised, and challenged, at various levels. The chapters will address, in turn, the rethinking of the UK's diplomatic, military, and imperial relationships across the globe; the ideological battles around the pursuit of economic growth; the debates about the welfare state, and what the nation should provide for its citizens; the increasingly insistent calls from Scotland and Wales to gain greater control over their own destinies, and from Northern Ireland to provide a peaceful solution to its internal divides; the attempts of protest groups and social movements to challenge the status quo; and the rise of a more secular, mediated, and consumerist society in which individuals had higher expectations of defining their lives. By peeling back and studying these different layers, we can start to understand the political contests that have shaped the post-war UK. How could the UK reconcile the legacies of its past with public expectations for the future? Was it possible for those who wanted to reform the UK to overcome deeply entrenched attitudes and power structures? How could politicians govern a more diverse and demanding population?

# 1
# Seeking a Role

The Second World War saw the UK achieve victory at huge human, financial, and material cost. In the immediate afterglow of Germany's surrender, the focus was understandably upon the heroism and resilience of UK citizens rather than the damage that had been done to the sinews of national power. 'We were the first, in this ancient island, to draw the sword against tyranny,' declared Prime Minister Winston Churchill in his VE (Victory in Europe) Day speech, as he applauded the tenacity of a nation that was forced to stand 'all alone for a whole year'. 'When shall the reputation and faith of this generation of English men and women fail?' he asked, in characteristically Anglocentric language. The answer, he concluded, was never: 'In the long years to come not only will the people of this island but of the world, wherever the bird of freedom chirps in human hearts, look back to what we've done.'[1] Churchill was very deliberately celebrating and updating the glorious chronicle of UK history, and left little room for the contributions of the empire in support of 'this ancient island'.

Three years later, as Conservative Party leader in opposition rather than prime minister, Churchill remained confident about the UK's future world role.

In an influential speech to a Conservative Party meeting in Llandudno, he argued that the UK had a vital, and irreplaceable, position in the international system because it stood 'at the very point of junction' of 'three great circles among the free nations and democracies', namely the Commonwealth and empire, the English-speaking world, and Europe:

> [W]e are the only country which has a great part in every one of them . . . here in this Island at the centre of the seaways and perhaps of the airways also, we have the opportunity of joining them all together. If we rise to the occasion in the years that are to come it may be found that once again we hold the key to opening a safe and happy future to humanity, and will gain for ourselves gratitude and fame.[2]

By the time Churchill delivered these words, in October 1948, this view of the UK as the pivot of the world order was already becoming hard to sustain. A dangerous gap was opening up between the rhetoric of the UK's political leaders and the nation's geopolitical and economic reality. The UK had been forced to concede independence to India and Pakistan, leaving the subcontinent in violent turmoil amidst the chaos of partition. It was increasingly difficult to maintain imperial authority after the wartime defeats in Asia, the rise of anti-colonial resistance, and an ever more influential rhetoric of national self-determination. The UK's finances were desperately precarious, and the

Treasury clung to the lifeline offered by loans and grants from the United States. Perhaps most fundamentally of all, as a new 'Cold War' emerged between the atom-bomb-wielding United States and a Soviet Union that had control of much of Eastern Europe, there were signs that the UK was going to be a junior partner in the diplomatic contest between the superpowers, not one of the main players.

How the United Kingdom should reposition itself in this new world order, and how it should reconcile its past as the world's greatest power with the realities of the present and future, were questions that politicians, diplomats, and the UK public all struggled to answer in the decades after 1945. The range and scope of the UK's relationships – Churchill's three circles – may have underpinned its global power in the nineteenth century, but they could easily become a heavy burden. Unlike their counterparts in defeated nations such as Germany or Japan, the UK's policy-makers were not forced to answer hard questions about their country's place in the world. Convinced that all three sets of relationships – with Europe, the United States, and the Commonwealth – were essential elements of the UK's greatness, they hedged, balanced, and kept their options open. The aim was to retain influence in all three, but many international partners became increasingly frustrated by the UK's lack of strategic clarity and commitment.

A number of commentators have interpreted the UK's departure from the European Union (EU) in 2020 as the sign of a deluded, nostalgic nation wanting to pursue global aspirations more befitting of its former status rather than gracefully adapting to the realities of its current diplomatic and economic situation. This is too simplistic. The UK was not as blinkered as this account suggests. There were many important voices in politics, business, and higher education keen to recast the UK's connections to Europe and the wider world, and powerful economic and social constituencies, including the City, and the sport and entertainment sectors, that embraced and drove such connections. The UK of 2020 was, in many respects, far more open, global, and tolerant than it was at the end of the war.

The real problem was that political and cultural elites struggled to develop a persuasive and attractive narrative that could connect the UK's past with its present and future. Not only did the glories of the Second World War become such a touchstone for the UK's political and popular culture, it was a particular version of that history that took hold: the Churchillian narrative that emphasized the UK's peculiar achievements and virtues, rather than the support it had received from its dominions and colonies, or its role as part of a broader international coalition. The mythology of national greatness made clear self-appraisal much harder, and made it much more difficult to commit decisively to any of the diplomatic options realistically available, and particularly to the emerging European Community. If many leading politicians believed that the UK's interests were best served by being part of the European project, few convincingly articulated a redefined role for the UK as a European power. In the absence of positive, forward-looking narratives, it was tempting for those disillusioned with the present to look back to the glories of the past, and take their lessons from there.

## *Recovering from War, Reviving Empire*

The immediate challenge in 1945 was to re-establish the equilibrium of a nation and empire that had been severely unbalanced by the pressures of war. Some difficult decisions had to be taken to ensure that the UK would recover the stature of a great power. Most pressing was addressing the dire financial situation. The debts generated by the military endeavour were colossal. Two world wars in a generation had transformed the UK from being the world's biggest creditor to its largest debtor. When, on the defeat of Japan, the United States abruptly cancelled the 'Lend-Lease' agreement that had underwritten wartime borrowing, the UK faced, in the words of leading economist John Maynard Keynes, a 'financial Dunkirk'. Keynes himself was dispatched to Washington to negotiate a new deal, and although a $3.75 billion loan was eventually agreed, supplemented three years later by substantial payments from the Europe-wide 'Marshall Aid' programme, the UK's financial position remained precarious, and reliant, as never before, on American goodwill. The UK's economic infrastructure had not suffered as much damage through invasion and military destruction as many of its European counterparts, and in the post-war years all possible industrial capacity was focused on production for export to stabilize the pound and reduce the deficit. The yearnings of UK consumers had to wait until global financial credibility was restored.

The war had also fundamentally damaged the authority that the UK wielded over parts of its empire. If the desperate retreat from Dunkirk in 1940 had been turned into a heroic narrative of defiant escape, there could be no disguising the humiliation of the defeats in the UK's Asian empire. The loss of Singapore to Japan in February 1942, with 130,000 British troops surrendering to a less numerous, but more dynamic, invading force, was the most dramatic reverse in recent UK history. Within weeks, Rangoon had also fallen as the Japanese swept into Burma. By August 1945, the Allies had finally defeated Japan, but it was clear that there could be no return to the pre-war status quo. This was the case also in India, where, faced with a mass civil disobedience campaign, the UK was only able to maintain control with coercive measures and the imprisonment of thousands of activists. Realizing that it no longer had the power to resist the calls for Indian self-determination, the government appointed Lord Montgomery as Viceroy to negotiate the UK's exit. The UK withdrew from the Indian subcontinent in August 1947 with little sense of responsibility for trying to secure a peaceful transition. Some 1 million people died, and 12 million were displaced, in the violence that accompanied the partition of the colonial territory into India and Pakistan. There was a similarly abrupt, and bloody, withdrawal from the British Mandate in Palestine. Unable to oversee a settlement between the Arab and Jewish protagonists, the UK disclaimed its mandate in November 1947 and did nothing to prevent a rapid slide to war. In both cases, the UK's world standing was damaged; Indian independence also led to a loss of imperial resources, notably military manpower, that significantly reduced the UK's ability to project its power in Asia.

Despite these severe pressures and forced concessions, the leading figures in the main political parties had very little desire to give up the UK's status as a great power with a global role. Military might was still a high priority, and the empire was certainly not considered to be dead – both just needed to be updated for a new era. This ambition was very clear in the pursuit of nuclear weaponry. The dropping of atomic bombs on Hiroshima and Nagasaki in August 1945 instantly changed the nature of warfare and the dynamics of international diplomacy. In the hard-headed calculations of military strategy, nations wielding the awesome power of nuclear technology inevitably attained a special status. This was an exclusive club that the UK was determined to join. When it became clear, in the immediate aftermath of the war, that the United States was ending the transatlantic scientific cooperation that had produced the first atomic weaponry – the 'Manhattan Project' – the Labour government decided to pursue its own version. In the infamous phrase of Ernest Bevin, the foreign secretary, the cabinet wanted a bomb with a 'bloody Union Jack' on it. This red, white, and blue bomb was developed with great secrecy, and at great cost, outside the normal structures of government, and marked the start of a long and difficult journey in pursuit of a viable and competitive independent deterrent. When the UK successfully tested a bomb in October 1952, the *Daily Express* rejoiced that 'Overnight it has restored Britain to the status of a major Power', so that the nation was no longer 'a weakling standing naked between American and Russian atomic might'.[3] The financial and technical difficulties were less important than the underlying statement of intent. Possession of the bomb was seen as a sign of national virility and was simply, Churchill argued, in full support of Labour's policy, 'the price we pay to sit at the top table'.[4]

The pursuit of nuclear weaponry was merely one part of a wider investment in what the historian David Edgerton has aptly termed the 'warfare state'.[5] Despite the UK's perilous financial situation, money could be found to maintain and project military power around the world. Conscription was enforced for the first time in peace. All British men were obliged to undergo a period of national service on turning eighteen, which enabled the UK to meet its military commitments in Europe, notably occupying part of defeated Germany, and across the empire, where resources were stretched now that Indian troops could not be deployed. The prospect of renewed conflict remained very real as the global rivalry between the United States and the Soviet Union escalated into a 'Cold War'. The UK aligned itself firmly with the United States, signing in April 1949 the Washington Treaty that created NATO as a collective security system of North American and European nations. Sharing the United States' desire to limit the spread of communism, between 1950 and 1953 the UK participated in the Korean War, seeking to support the regime in the south against Soviet- and China-backed northern forces. By the time the conflict ended in stalemate in 1953, over 1,000 UK soldiers had been killed. The costs of this global military apparatus were huge. In the early 1950s, the UK's defence expenditure was around 10% of the nation's GDP, significantly higher than it had been immediately before the First or Second World War.[6] Even with this level of spending, however, the UK could not hope to keep up with the superpowers of the United States and the Soviet Union.

The great power mindset was retained in relation to the empire and the Commonwealth. The loss of India did not weaken the tenacity of the UK's hold on its empire, even if there was often now an updated rhetoric accompanying it, based on 'modernization' and 'trusteeship'. It was widely believed that territories in Africa and Asia were not yet 'ready' for independence, and in the Cold War environment the United States and the UK shared an anxiety about colonies turning to communism. In London, governments promoted schemes of imperial development and resource extraction that would improve the UK's financial position, and were prepared to use its military might to preserve these resources from internal or external threats. Malaya, for example, provided valuable commodities like rubber and tin, and local uprisings against the colonial regime were met with often brutal force. In Kenya, UK soldiers killed over 10,000 Mau Mau rebels between 1952 and 1960 in a counter-insurgency operation that also saw the extensive use of torture, detention, and aerial bombing. Racist stereotypes about irrational and uncivilized local populations remained prevalent among colonial officials and military forces.

The most visible, and consequential, intervention came in Egypt. Egypt had actually secured its independence in 1922, but the UK had retained a significant military presence, mainly to protect its strategic interests in the Anglo-French-owned Suez Canal. This UK influence was becoming increasingly insecure with the rise to the presidency of Gamal Abdel Nasser, who embodied the forces of Egyptian nationalism and anti-imperial sentiment. Although a deal for UK military withdrawal was agreed in 1954, Nasser's decision in July 1956 to nationalize the Suez Canal was a bold challenge to the authority and economic interests of the UK and France. As the historian John Darwin has observed, 'Britain's ability to use the Canal Zone and its bases . . . was its greatest surviving geostrategic asset outside the Home Islands', and was the essential underpinning for a Middle Eastern role that 'lifted Britain out of the category of a merely European power'.[7] Failing to challenge Nasser's actions would be tantamount to accepting a substantial downgrading of the UK's great power status, and for Prime Minister Anthony Eden, who viewed the crisis through the prism of the Second World War, it was not in the national interest to appease dictators. With negotiations failing to resolve the crisis, the UK and France concocted – in conditions of absolute secrecy – a plan with Israel in which an Israeli attack on Egypt would provide the pretext for military intervention to secure the canal zone. The Eden government, insufficiently clear-sighted about the UK's declining power in the world, gravely miscalculated how such an intervention would be received by the United States and international opinion through the United Nations. When UK and French troops landed in Egypt in November, criticism was immediate and ferocious. An emergency session of the UN General Assembly approved a ceasefire resolution, and in the conspicuous absence of US support, the pound was dangerously undermined on the financial markets as speculators piled in to sell the currency. The UK could not resist this combination of moral and economic pressure, and military forces were withdrawn, to be replaced by UN peacekeepers. Eden, suffering from ill-health, resigned, although not before lying to the House of Commons about his complicity in the conspiracy with France and Israel. The UK had been humiliated.

The Suez débâcle inevitably altered how the UK was perceived, internally and externally. The nation looked at itself in the mirror, and could not avoid seeing flaws and frailties. It was clear that the UK could no longer make significant and controversial global interventions without the support, or at least acquiescence, of the United States; this recognition shaped foreign policy for decades to come. The UK's self-image as a moral leader was badly tarnished, and critics of the complacency and insularity of the nation's 'establishment' had been supplied with powerful ammunition. Yet it is important not to exaggerate the extent to which Suez marked a turning point. The UK was not going to give up its global pretensions lightly, nor were entrenched patterns of thought about national greatness going to fade quickly. Broadcasting to the nation a week after replacing Eden as prime minister, Harold Macmillan dismissed the notion that the UK was in a spiral of decline:

> Every now and again since the war I have heard people say: 'Isn't Britain only a second- or third-class power now? Isn't she on the way out?' What nonsense! This is a great country, and do not let us be ashamed to say so . . . do not let us have any more

defeatist talk of second-class powers and of dreadful things to come. Britain has been great, is great, and will stay great, provided we close our ranks and get on with the job.[8]

Although the Suez intervention caused significant divisions in the country, once Eden had resigned, the political storm soon abated, and Macmillan worked to re-establish relations with the United States, and to reassure the UK public that little had changed. As would become evident, however, Suez was an indication of deeper geopolitical forces that would force the UK to make significant shifts in policy.

## *From Empire to Europe*

In the decade or so after the end of the Second World War, the UK had tried to preserve its great power status and role. There had been some concessions (notably accepting the independence of India and Pakistan), and several attempts to adapt to military and geopolitical change (pursuing nuclear weaponry and trying to 'modernize' empire), but there had not really been a fundamental rethinking of the UK's place in the world. In the late 1950s and early 1960s, however, it became apparent that clinging onto the status quo was no longer a credible option. The world was changing, and the UK had to make some difficult choices. The actions of President Nasser were manifestations of a broader wave of nationalism and anti-colonialism in Africa, Asia, and the Middle East that would not be contained by piecemeal reforms. Political movements demanding independence grew in strength and challenged all the major colonial powers, including France and Belgium, as well as the UK. Any military responses to such movements would be bloody, tactically risky, and very hard to sustain. The highly publicized example of Algeria drove this point home with painful clarity. French attempts to counter the Algerian National Liberation Front (FLN) between 1954 and 1962 led to considerable loss of life and internal political turmoil without producing any successful resolution; peace was only achieved with the granting of independence. Defending colonialism seemed akin to stemming the tides of history.

At the same time, the European recovery from the Second World War moved into a rebuilding phase that posed fresh questions for the UK. Beginning with the Schuman declaration of May 1950, which proposed a joint European Coal and Steel Community, France and Germany drove forward the idea of European cooperation and collaboration as the only way to overcome the geopolitical enmities that had wreaked devastation on the continent twice in two generations. UK governments, still keen to pursue a global role that, it was believed, fundamentally distinguished the nation from other European powers, showed little enthusiasm for these initiatives. In May 1957, Germany, France, Italy, Belgium, Luxembourg, and the Netherlands signed the Treaty of Rome, which established the European Economic Community (EEC) and set out the ambition of achieving 'ever closer union'. By standing aside from these negotiations and the eventual agreement, the UK lost the opportunity at this initial stage to shape the nature of the EEC and influence the direction of travel towards closer union; it confirmed an existing suspicion that it did not see its interests as being firmly entwined with the nations of Western Europe.

The UK did participate, in May 1960, in the establishment of the European Free Trade Association (EFTA) incorporating seven non-EEC countries (Austria, Denmark, Norway, Portugal, Sweden, Switzerland, and the UK), but this did not convey the same economic benefits as EEC membership and reinforced the nation's position as part of an 'outer ring' around the core European project. By the end of the 1950s, moreover, there were increasing anxieties that the UK's economy was being outperformed by many of the EEC nations, and particularly Germany. The civil service 'Future Policy Study 1960–70', produced in February 1960, warned of the dangers of the UK being strategically and financially overcommitted, and noted that the 'basic rule of British policy is clear: we must never allow ourselves to be put in a position where we have to make a final choice between the United States and Europe'.[9] Although the study did not directly contemplate joining the EEC, as long as entry into Europe did not threaten the Atlantic alliance, it was likely to become an increasingly attractive option in the face of the UK's strategic challenges.

Over the course of the 1960s, these countervailing pressures led to a dramatic reorientation of UK foreign policy, marked by a retreat from empire, a significant reduction in conventional military capacity, and a pivot towards Europe. The symbolic end of empire can be dated to Harold Macmillan's speech in February 1960 to the South African Houses of Parliament, in which he famously observed that the 'wind of change' was blowing through Africa, marked, in particular, by 'the growth of national consciousness'. No sensible politician could stand in the way of these powerful forces, he argued: 'We must all accept it as a fact, and our national policies must take account of it.'[10] The moral and ideological underpinnings of empire had snapped, and an economically and strategically overstretched nation could do little more than secure a relatively peaceful transition of power to local elites. By 1960, independence had already been granted to Ghana and Malaya, and over the coming years nations across the full spread of the British Empire broke free, including in Africa (Nigeria, Uganda, Kenya, Gambia, Sierra Leone, Tanzania), Asia (Singapore, the Maldives), the Mediterranean (Cyprus, Malta), the Caribbean (Jamaica, Trinidad and Tobago, Barbados), the Middle East (Aden), and Oceania (Western Samoa). This was accompanied by a phased reduction of military capacity, with the end of National Service in 1963 and the announcement in January 1968 of a withdrawal from all bases east of Suez. There were territories where a suitable exit could not be negotiated or was not deemed appropriate – Rhodesia, Hong Kong, the Falkland Islands – and there was a continued celebration of the Commonwealth as a multinational association of like-minded nations, but there was no doubt that the imperial game was over.

Macmillan's plan was that imperial retreat would be mirrored by an advance into the EEC. In 1962, he carefully persuaded his party to support a formal application to join 'the Six' as a means of reinvigorating the economy and deepening continental relationships. With the UK's global influence receding, pursuing its strategic interests through a relationship with Europe seemed to be an attractive option. Dean Acheson, the former US secretary of state, set out these calculations in more unforgiving terms when he famously remarked in December 1962 that the UK had 'lost an empire and not yet found a role'. 'Britain's attempt to play a separate power role,' he continued, 'that is, a role apart from Europe, a role based on a "special relationship" with the United States, a role based on being the head of a Commonwealth . . . this role is about played out.' He argued that Britain's application to join the EEC, by contrast, was a 'decisive turning point', and suggested that if its application was accepted, a 'step forward of vast importance will have been taken'.[11] Empire was the past, and Europe should be the future. But resetting the UK's relationship with Europe was by no means straightforward. The issue was politically divisive at home. Hugh Gaitskell, the Labour leader, declared in October 1962 that joining the EEC would mean the 'end of Britain as an independent European state . . . the end of a thousand years of history . . . [and] the end of the Commonwealth', and thus started several decades of controversy about the relationship with Europe.[12] More pertinently in the short term, EEC members were not prepared to embrace the UK's overtures. Charles de Gaulle, the French president, was adamant that the UK did not truly see itself as a European nation, and would be an unwelcome agent of US influence in the community. De Gaulle vetoed the application in January 1963, as he did again in 1968 when Harold Wilson, Gaitskell's successor as Labour leader, persuaded his party that a second application was in the nation's best interests. The UK ended the 1960s with a much-reduced global reach, and still adrift in Europe.

It was only with the resignation of de Gaulle in 1969, and the election the following year of Edward Heath, a genuinely Europhile prime minister, that the balance of European Community opinion tilted finally in the UK's favour. Heath made joining the EEC his administration's priority, and he managed to win over de Gaulle's successor, Georges Pompidou, and other sceptics in Europe. Parliament passed the necessary legislation – with both the Conservatives and Labour internally divided over the issue – and the UK joined the EEC, alongside Ireland and Denmark, on 1 January 1973. The political disputes were not yet over. When Harold Wilson was re-elected prime minister in 1974, the only way he could manage the splits in his party was to renegotiate the terms and offer a referendum on the decision to stay in Europe. This was a momentous decision: not only was it the UK's first national referendum, it enshrined the principle that significant issues of national sovereignty should be put to the electorate. Persuading the British people about the merits of British foreign policy was now critical. The Conservative, Labour, and Liberal front benches, alongside a broad spectrum of press and business opinion, campaigned for a 'Yes' vote, and won, in June 1975 a straightforward victory, with 67% in favour of membership on a turnout of 64%. The UK, it seemed, was firmly in Europe.

It is tempting to create a narrative that the 1960s and 1970s witnessed a smooth transition of the UK from an imperial to a European nation. The withdrawal from empire, with a few notable exceptions, was achieved relatively peacefully and seemed to cause minimal discontent amongst the UK public. At the same time, the accession to Europe was strongly endorsed in a high-profile vote. In reality, however, these shifts were far less clear cut. While the UK public might have accepted the loss of the empire with relative equanimity, the patterns of thought entrenched by centuries of imperial rule were far more deeply embeddeded than many recognized. The anxieties created by the immigration into the UK from the former empire made that very clear. Ideas of British superiority, of racial hierarchies, of the right of the UK to intervene around the globe, were very resilient. At the same time, the resounding victory in the 1975 referendum did not indicate that the public was converted to the European project. Joining Europe was largely sold in pragmatic terms as an economic benefit to a nation that was struggling to maintain its economic competitiveness and needed, in Acheson's words, to 'find a role'. Few leading politicians matched Heath's commitment to the EEC, and UK politics and popular culture continued to be oriented to the United States and the Commonwealth as much as they were to Europe. Once the referendum campaign had concluded, few were willing to take up the task of 'selling' Europe to the UK public, and for many people, knowledge of, and enthusiasm for, the EEC remained superficial.

## *Retaining a Global Role*

The continuing power of imperial beliefs and global entanglements was conspicuous under Margaret Thatcher, who became prime minister in the Conservative Party election victory of 1979, and retained office until her resignation in 1990. Thatcher argued that in the post-war decades the UK had lost touch with the values that had made it successful, and had too timidly accepted decline. She unapologetically resurrected the rhetoric of national greatness, reaffirmed the importance of the Cold War alliance with the United States, and maintained a conspicuously transactional approach to Europe. Thatcher was too much of a realist to stand in the way of decolonization where it had momentum: her government in 1980 reached an agreement to the long-running Rhodesian problem that led to the independence of Zimbabwe, and in 1984 she signed a deal that would see Hong Kong return to Chinese rule in 1997. At the same time, she was unafraid to be forceful in the protection of what she perceived to be the UK's national interests. This was most evident in the 1982 Falklands War, which ultimately cemented her international reputation and transformed her political fortunes. When Argentina, under the rule of General Galtieri's military junta, asserted its historical claim to the Falkland Islands (Malvinas) through an invasion, Thatcher took the gamble of assembling a taskforce to carry out an inevitably risky military response. The territories themselves had little value – the Argentine author Jorge Luis Borges memorably compared the conflict to 'two bald men fighting over a comb' – but retaining them became a test of national identity. Supported by boisterously jingoistic popular newspapers such as the *Sun* and the *Daily Mail*, Thatcher dodged controversies around elements of the military engagements, such as the sinking of the Argentine cruiser *General Belgrano*, and claimed that the eventual retaking of the islands demonstrated that the UK had 'ceased to be a nation in retreat'. Addressing a Conservative Party rally in Cheltenham in July 1982, in the immediate aftermath of victory, she declared that:

> When we started out, there were the waverers and the fainthearts. The people who thought that Britain could no longer seize the initiative for herself. The people who thought we could no longer do the great things which we once did. Those who believed that our decline was irreversible – that we could never again be what we were . . . that Britain was no longer the nation that had built an Empire and ruled a quarter of the world. Well they were wrong. The lesson of the Falklands is that Britain has not changed and that this nation still has those sterling qualities which shine through our history.[13]

The real significance of the Falklands War was the renewed legitimacy it gave to the language of nationalism and imperial nostalgia. Thatcher was chided in some quarters for glorifying military success – the Archbishop of Canterbury, Robert Runcie, pointedly remembered the bereaved on both sides in his sermon at the Falklands Thanksgiving service – but her success in the general election the following year indicated the wider appeal of this patriotic rhetoric. These noisy invocations of national virility made it difficult to have sober and hard-headed conversations about the realities of the UK's global role.

Thatcher adopted a similarly combative approach in her dealings with Europe. Although a supporter of Community membership in the 1975 referendum, she did little to disguise her diplomatic suspicions of France and Germany when she became prime minister, and her vision of beneficial European integration was firmly market-based and UK-centric. Adamant that the nation was not getting good value from its membership, in 1984 she abrasively negotiated a rebate on the UK's contribution to European finances. Thatcher was happy to support the Single European Act of 1986, because its creation of a single European market promised economic dividends for the UK, but the prospect of further political integration, and particularly the interventionist social policies proposed by Jacques Delors, president of the European Commission, was anathema. In a speech to the College of Europe in Bruges in September 1988, Thatcher outlined her determination to see 'willing and active cooperation between independent sovereign states' rather than any attempts to 'suppress nationhood and concentrate power at the centre of a European conglomerate'. 'We have not successfully rolled back the frontiers of the state in Britain,' she continued, 'only to see them re-imposed at a European level with a European super-state exercising a new dominance from Brussels.'[14] The 'Bruges speech', and Thatcher's increasingly tetchy relationship with Europe, alienated several leading Cabinet members, including Nigel Lawson and Geoffrey Howe; her opposition to joining the European Exchange Rate Mechanism (ERM), which sought to align European currencies, and her scepticism towards German reunification played a significant role in her eventual fall from power. On the back benches, though, the speech helped to crystallize Eurosceptic feeling and would be very influential in shaping the Conservative Party's approach to Europe in the decades to come. John Major, Thatcher's successor as prime minister, managed to obtain parliamentary approval for the 1992 Maastricht Treaty, the next phase of European integration, but only after securing opt-outs in key areas – notably from plans to join the euro, the proposed common currency, and from the protocol on the Social Chapter, covering legislation on working conditions – and enduring a damaging guerrilla campaign in the House of Commons from opponents within his party. During its first two decades in what was now the EU, the UK had been an awkward partner and had done little to generate popular enthusiasm for integration.

The fall of the Berlin Wall in 1989, and the subsequent collapse of the Soviet Union, led to some euphoric celebrations of Western democracy, even if the wars that broke out in the Balkans in 1991 were a reminder that this was not the 'end of history'. The UK's financial sector, in particular, benefited from the wave of globalization and deregulation that marked the 1990s, and the opening in 1994 of the Channel Tunnel between Folkestone and Calais, and the rise in the mid-1990s of budget airlines such as Ryanair and EasyJet, ensured that individual mobility was easier than ever before. The introduction of the

World Wide Web, and the growing reach of internet browsers and websites for everyday use, generated a powerful new form of global interconnection. Yet if the UK was becoming, in some respects, more mobile and outward-facing than ever before, there was little sign that it had fully come to terms with the changed realities of its global position. Politicians, social commentators, and cultural producers struggled to produce compelling narratives about the UK's place in the world, with the result that traditional motifs retained their influence. Narratives based around the Second World War continued to hold considerable sway, conspicuously shaping popular and political perceptions of Europe, especially Germany. ('Achtung Surrender!' declared the front page of the *Daily Mirror* on the eve of England's football match against Germany in the 1996 European Championship.) While Thatcher's personal rapport with US President Reagan added lustre to transatlantic diplomacy, and the UK threw considerable military weight into the US-led operations in the 1990–1 Gulf War (fought in response to the Iraqi invasion of Kuwait), there could be little pretence that the 'special relationship' was one between equals. Ongoing military and intelligence cooperation with the United States did not necessarily produce significant diplomatic advantages to the UK. The Commonwealth had lost its prestige, and Australia and Canada looked far more to the United States than the UK. The persistence of racism indicated that many struggled to accept the multicultural society that was the inevitable outcome of the UK's imperial entanglements. Tony Blair's New Labour government, elected in 1997, tried to update national identity around the motifs of cultural vibrancy with its 'Cool Britannia' campaign, but this gained limited traction. Relative economic prosperity, even if it was unequally shared, ensured that by the turn of the millennium narratives of national decline had lost the resonance they had in the 1970s, but there were few compelling visions of the UK's future place in the world.

The events of 9/11 – a series of attacks organized by the radical Islamist group Al-Qaeda, which saw planes flown into the Twin Towers of New York's World Trade Center, and into the Pentagon in Arlington County, Virginia – shattered the diplomatic optimism of the 1990s. Blair immediately declared the UK's intention to stand 'shoulder to shoulder' with the United States as it waged a 'War on Terror', and the UK joined the subsequent US-led military operations in Afghanistan, where the Taliban leadership was accused of harbouring Al-Qaeda fighters. Blair had argued in a speech in Chicago in April 1999 that there were circumstances – such as the attempted ethnic cleansing of Muslims in Kosovo, where the UK had recently joined a NATO-led bombing campaign against Serbian forces – that justified military action, and over the coming years he would use the doctrine of liberal interventionism to defend the use of force against rogue regimes. This was an updated and moralized version of the UK's global role. Although he was able to maintain broad support for a muscular policy in Kosovo and Afghanistan, Blair's backing of US President George W. Bush's plans to invade Saddam Hussein's Iraq was hugely controversial. Eager to find an unimpeachable rationale for intervention, given there was little to connect Iraq to the 9/11 attacks, Blair encouraged the United States to take its case to the United Nations. The UN agreed to send in a team of weapons inspectors, led by Swedish diplomat Hans Blix, to investigate the alleged Iraqi programme to create weapons of mass destruction (WMD). The failure to find incontrovertible evidence of such a programme led to splits in the UN, making it impossible to pass a second resolution to the UK explicitly authorizing war. The UK joined the US-led invasion in March 2003 regardless: for Blair, remaining close to America in its fight against 'evil' regimes ultimately trumped other political considerations.

The Iraq war divided the British public like no military action since Suez. Over a million people joined an anti-war march in London, and Blair secured approval for the war in the House of Commons only in the teeth of significant opposition across his party. The initial military successes – Baghdad fell within three weeks – seemed to vindicate military action, but no WMD were located, and the inability to restore stability exposed the lack of a robust plan for longer-term reconstruction and peace-building. As UK military losses continued to mount, Blair was accused of taking the UK to war under a false prospectus.

The divisions over the war and its legacy corroded his reputation and were immensely damaging to the Labour Party. The UK finally withdrew combat troops from Iraq in 2011, and from Afghanistan in 2014, but both countries remained in turmoil. When the United States withdrew its forces from Afghanistan in August 2021, alongside the remaining UK training and advisory missions, the Taliban immediately retook control of the capital, Kabul. It was hard to see the final result as anything less than a humiliation for Western hubris. The wars did not seem to make the world a safer place, because Western military interventions provided fresh motivation for terrorism. On 7 July 2005, radical Islamists killed fifty-two people in central London with a series of bombs on underground trains and a bus. Subsequent years would see a series of similar incidents, not just in the UK but across Europe, Africa, and the Middle East. The UK did not immediately lose its appetite for foreign interventions, joining in 2011 a NATO-led mission in Libya which eventually overthrew long-time leader Muammar Gaddafi, but it was significant that in 2013 the House of Commons refused to support Prime Minister David Cameron's proposed intervention in the Syrian civil war. Politicians and the public were becoming disillusioned with the human, economic, and moral costs of military actions that produced very uncertain outcomes. The post-Cold War hopes for a new liberal world order had long disappeared.

## The Challenge of Euroscepticism

If the UK's role in the wider world was brought into question by the interventions in Afghanistan and Iraq, so too was its place in the project of European integration increasingly subject to debate. Tony Blair's Labour government was keen to develop more positive European relationships after the tensions of the Thatcher and Major years, but it was not prepared to join the new European single currency (the euro) introduced in 1999, and therefore remained detached from the central processes driving integration. Its positive but pragmatic approach appealed to the political centre ground and ensured that vehemently anti-EU groups such as the United Kingdom Independence Party (UKIP, formed from the Anti-Federalist League in 1993) remained on the margins. Conservative attempts to appeal to voters with campaigns to 'save the pound' equally gained little traction. But two developments in the new century would give considerable momentum to the forces of Euroscepticism. In 2004, when the EU admitted ten countries from Eastern and Central Europe, the Labour government decided not to impose any transitional controls on the free movement of labour. Blair was a firm believer in the benefits of globalization and argued that migrant workers 'make Britain not weaker but stronger'. The scale of immigration – around 800,000 people entered the UK from the newly acceded countries in the five years after 2004

– was unexpected and gave political opportunities to those who wanted to claim that Eastern Europeans were 'taking' UK jobs and putting local communities under unprecedented pressure. 'If I could connect open-door immigration and leaving the EU,' recalled Nigel Farage, the driving force behind UKIP, 'that was the magic bullet. Ever since 2004, that was the argument I made.'[15]

These anxieties became far more pressing after the recession caused by the financial crash of 2007–8. As living standards stagnated and government-led austerity reduced welfare benefits and cut local authority budgets, it became increasingly plausible to connect social and economic problems to the strains caused by immigration and the policy failures of the EU. This is where the UK's long-term political ambivalence to European integration became a problem. With so few prominent political and cultural voices prepared to offer full-blooded support for Europe, rather than a pragmatic and functional approval, Eurosceptic voices were able to get a wide and often unchallenged hearing. Alarmed by the growing electoral support for UKIP, and seeking to appease the right wing of his own Conservative Party, Prime Minister David Cameron promised in 2013 that a future Conservative government would renegotiate the UK's terms of EU membership and put them to a referendum. When the Conservatives unexpectedly won an overall majority in the general election of 2015, the journey to referendum was set.

The victory of the 'Leave' campaign in June 2016, by a margin of 51.9% to 48.1%, shocked the political elites at Westminster – all the major parties had supported 'Remain' – and throughout the EU. The results revealed a divided nation, with younger, university-educated, and affluent voters more likely to support 'Remain', and London, Scotland, and Northern Ireland the areas most in favour of staying in the EU. As the geographer Danny Dorling has noted, however, most people who voted Leave, in absolute terms, lived in southern England, and 59% of them were middle class. This was a broad-based revolt, with many different motivations, and not just a response of the 'left behind'.[16] Ultimately it revealed that significant sections of the country believed that the EU made little difference to their lives, and were confident that the UK could act in the world more successfully on its own. This was not necessarily a nostalgia for the past – although that was clearly a strong element for some – but it did reflect a widely held sense that the UK's history had made it a global player that could, and should, operate beyond the constraints of Europe. Ironically, a deep commitment to Europe was perhaps most visible after the referendum as Remainers mobilized to try to prevent departure or force another referendum. The popular decision had been made, however, and once Boris Johnson, the leader of the Leave campaign, became prime minister in 2019, he won a general election, secured an exit deal, and the UK left the EU on 31 January 2020.

The 'Global Britain' that Johnson promoted in the wake of departure had more than faint echoes of Churchill's 'three circles'. The UK wanted the best of all worlds: a 'special relationship' with the United States; the benefits of extensive global trading connections with the Commonwealth and beyond; and also extensive interactions with the neighbouring European market. The 'Aukus' security pact, signed with the United States and Australia in September 2021, offered a sign of the UK's future strategic direction as it looked beyond the EU. But Johnson's confidence that the UK could have it all – he famously described his 'policy on cake' as 'pro having it and pro eating it' – smacked of the exceptionalism that had characterized so much of UK policy-making since 1945 and before, rather than a coherent vision of the future that had accepted what the country could actually achieve. With the Office for Budget Responsibility predicting in October 2021 that leaving the EU would reduce the UK's potential GDP by 4%, critics argued that there would simply be less cake available. Fifty years after Dean Acheson accused the UK of struggling to find a role, it was not clear that much progress had been made.

# 2

# The Pursuit of Economic Growth

In 1945, it appeared that a century and more of UK global economic success was coming to an end. Huge debts forced the government to maintain rationing and austerity measures into peacetime to stabilize the nation's finances. Mobilizing the military machine in two world wars had been eye-wateringly expensive, and required the sale of countless overseas assets. Heavy bombardment during the Blitz had not only killed some 60,000 civilians, but also destroyed infrastructure, housing, and business premises; many towns and cities needed extensive repair and rebuilding. The export industries that had underpinned the UK's prosperity in the nineteenth century – textiles, mining, iron and steel, shipbuilding – were all struggling to cope with more intense competition, often from rivals which had invested in more advanced machinery and more streamlined processes. The economic dislocations of the inter-war years had scarred many areas of the UK, especially in northern England, central Scotland, South Wales, and Northern Ireland. The bitter memories of the hardship of mass unemployment and the pressing desire for a more secure future were key factors propelling Clement Attlee's Labour Party to power in 1945. The UK could not rest on former laurels and the time had come, it seemed, for radical change.

Labour's bold manifesto, 'Let us Face the Future', exuded confidence that the party had the vision and the tools to rebuild the economy and renew growth. At the heart of this reconstruction would be an active and interventionist state. Wartime victory helped to legitimize the ideas of state planning and economic management that had been developed by John Maynard Keynes, amongst others, over the previous decade. The nationalization of key industries would enable more efficient organization and coordination, while governments would use fiscal levers, such as interest rates and taxation levels, to stimulate or dampen demand and sustain employment. Governments took on the responsibility of generating growth and prosperity more explicitly than ever before, in the process raising the expectations of electors and placing the economy at the heart of the political battle. In the quarter century after the war, many of these promises seemed to be realized, at least for ordinary citizens across the UK experiencing unprecedented rises in real wages, new consumer opportunities, and greater job security. Yet this prosperity was as much due to favourable global conditions as expert governance. As the world economy destabilized from the 1970s, politicians, economists, and entrepreneurs increasingly questioned the effectiveness of Keynesian solutions and state planning. It was difficult for any government to manage long-term economic restructuring caused by the declining competitiveness of many of the UK's heavy industries, the rise of the retail and service sectors, and dramatic shifts in communications and technology. These deeper realignments made it harder to 'face the future' than it had seemed in 1945. 'Modernization' was never straightforward.

The UK's economic performance continued to be shaped by the legacies of the past, notably the geographical concentrations of activity produced by industrialization; the trading relationships shaped by empire (including the profits of slavery); the legal and cultural frameworks governing business management and industrial relations; and the entrenched political, financial, and administrative power of London. As the economy faltered in the 1970s, politicians also took inspiration from the past to explain and justify their economic strategies. For Margaret Thatcher, 'rolling back the state' would enable a return to the dynamism of the Victorian era, while for Eurosceptics, leaving the EU would allow the UK to reinvigorate some of the global trading networks that had undergirded the empire. From the 1980s, the political triumph of right-wing economic policies ensured that in terms of inequality and the distribution of wealth, at least, the economy increasingly resembled the Edwardian period more than the Labour's mid-century 'New Jerusalem'. By the end of the twentieth century, moreover, it was becoming clear that the future would be shaped by the past in an even more dangerous way. Industrialized economies had devoured fossil fuels and degraded the environment with little thought for the long-term consequences. Affluence, advertising, and globalization encouraged a culture of consumption and waste that looked unsustainable as the realities of climate change started to bite. By the early 2020s, widespread political discussion of a 'green new deal', as well as the exploitation of artificial intelligence and new technologies, raised the prospect of another radical reconstruction of the economy.

## Planning, the State, and the Modern Economy

'The nation needs a tremendous overhaul, a great programme of modernisation and re-equipment,' declared Labour's 1945 manifesto. This could only be achieved 'by drastic policies of replanning and by keeping a firm constructive hand on our whole productive machinery'.[1] Having been given an unexpectedly large parliamentary majority, Attlee's government was able to implement many of these 'drastic policies'. The result was the most dramatic programme of economic reform the UK had ever witnessed. The coal industry, at the heart of British economic life and employing over 800,000 people, was nationalized. Hand-over ceremonies under fluttering Union flags were held to mark the occasion on 1 January 1947, with a message from the prime minister proudly declaring it 'one of the great days in the industrial history of our country'.[2] As well as coal, a range of other strategic sectors were brought under public control, notably transport (railways, road haulage, and civil aviation), power and communications (cable and wireless, electricity and gas), and, most controversially, iron and steel manufacture. The state took ownership of the Bank of England, enabling the government to appoint its governor and directors. In areas where the state was not taking direct control, there were new forms of intervention, planning, and regulation. The 1947 Town and Country Planning Act gave local authorities extensive powers to determine land use and to oversee ambitious reconstruction and public housing programmes (while also establishing green belts to limit the urban sprawl). This went hand in hand with efforts to ensure a more rational distribution of the population, including the creation of new towns to ease the pressures of overcrowding in growing conurbations. By the 1960s, this policy had led to the redevelopment of places like Bracknell, Crawley, Hemel Hempstead, Stevenage, Cumbernauld, and East Kilbride. There were also changes in the countryside. The 1947 Agriculture Act introduced a system of grants, subsidies, and price guarantees to stimulate domestic food production, while County Agricultural Executive Committees encouraged the consolidation of farm holdings to improve productivity. These extensions of central power came while the system of rationing of food, fuel, and consumer goods continued (and intensified with the restrictions on the purchase of bread between 1946 and 1948). It did now seem as if the government's hands were on the nation's 'whole productive machinery'.

These reforms were all motivated by a widespread belief, in the Labour Party and progressive opinion more broadly, that the state, with the right expertise, information, and coordination, could manage, direct, and integrate the economy more strategically and efficiently than the market, and that by doing so it could spread prosperity across the UK. This period saw, as the historian David Edgerton has argued, the emergence of a 'developmental state' creating a distinctively national economy, protected by tariffs and controls on the exchange of currency, and increasingly focusing on self-supply where that was feasible.[3] The UK continued, of course, to rely on global trading networks, particularly with the empire and Commonwealth, but the openness and *laissez-faire* attitudes of the late-Victorian and Edwardian periods had long gone. A notable marker of this shift in attitudes was the Conservative Party's acceptance of the main outlines of Labour's 'drastic policies' when it returned to power after the 1951 general election. The Conservatives privatized the iron and steel industry, along with parts of the road haulage sector, and made political capital from the ending of rationing in 1954. In general terms, however, the party accepted the new role of the state to manage the economy, generate growth, and preserve high levels of employment. While setting themselves against further nationalizations, the Conservative governments of the 1950s and early 1960s were content to maintain a sizeable public sector. Harold Macmillan, prime minister from

1957 to 1963, was an unapologetic proponent of planning, and in 1962 introduced both the National Economic Development Council (NEDC, or 'Neddy') and the National Incomes Commission (NIC, or 'Nicky') to strengthen the apparatus of central economic direction. 'Neddy' brought representatives from the government, business, and the trade unions to consider the latest economic information and to discuss national economic strategy, and reflected the Conservative government's recognition of the value of working with the unions as well as business leaders in developing policy. 'Nicky' assessed proposed wage settlements and was deemed a necessary tool for governments seeking to manage inflation. If the mechanisms and priorities changed over time and between parties – Harold Wilson's 1964 Labour government established a new Department of Economic Affairs to oversee a 'National Plan', and replaced 'Nicky' with a National Board for Prices and Incomes – there was a broad consensus that economic success in the modern world required an active and interventionist state.

Did these measures work? This is a complex and hugely contested question, not least because the answer has enormous policy consequences for contemporary discussions about the role of the state. At one level – the level of the average UK citizen of the 1950s and 1960s – the answer is yes. Although domestic rationing continued, the economic dislocation that followed the First World War was avoided, and the heavy industries that had been under severe pressure before the rearmament of the late 1930s now experienced a period of resurgence. There was no return of the mass unemployment of the 1930s, and unemployment rates did not rise above historic lows of 2–3% until the late 1960s. It was widely remarked that a worker could leave a job on a Friday and expect to walk into a new one the following week. Between 1950 and 1975, the UK's gross domestic product (GDP) doubled in real terms, the fastest sustained rate of growth the nation had ever experienced. This growth fed striking rises in average real wages, and, after rationing ended in the mid-1950s, powered a surge of consumer spending. New televisions, transistor radios, fridges, and washing machines transformed homes around the country, and the car now came within the reach of ordinary families. Young people had greater spending power than ever before, ensuring a boom for the popular music industry, fashion retailers, and coffee bars. Conservative Prime Minister Harold Macmillan famously captured this mood of affluence with his declaration to a political rally in Bedford in July 1957 that 'most of our people have never had it so good'. 'Go around the country,' he continued, 'go to the industrial towns, go to the farms and you will see a state of prosperity such as we have never had in my lifetime – nor indeed in the history of this country.'[4] It even seemed that these economic transformations were reshaping the political landscape. Macmillan's Conservatives, unashamedly taking the credit for the good times, achieved a commanding victory in the 1959 general election. After three consecutive electoral defeats, and signs that affluent and aspirational working-class voters were swinging to the Tories, some commentators wondered whether Labour would ever win power again.

When we put the UK in a wider frame of reference, however, the picture looks different. The post-war economic expansion was a global phenomenon, and the UK's growth rates were significantly lower than many of its competitors – including the defeated Germany and Japan. The UK struggled to maintain a positive balance of payments (the difference in value between payments flowing in and flowing out of the country), which put considerable pressure on the value of sterling, and forced governments periodically to restrain domestic spending by raising interest rates or taxation (lambasted by critics as 'Stop–Go' economics). Part of the strain on the national finances was caused by the high level of military spending that the UK maintained in peacetime: as a proportion of overall government expenditure, defence accounted for 23% in 1950, 24% in 1960, and 17% in 1970; only the United States spent more.[5] The costs of trying to preserve great power status were considerable, and weighed down the UK far more than many of its European counterparts. The economic orientation to the Commonwealth – still taking three-quarters of the UK's exports in 1956 – meant that UK firms failed to reap the rewards of more dynamic economic markets. At a time when Commonwealth partners turned increasingly to the United States and Asia, and decolonization ensured the loss of overseas assets, the UK also found itself outside Europe's new common market. In November 1967, Harold Wilson's Labour government was forced to devalue sterling by 14% to ease the intense pressure on the currency, and although the prime minister tried to reassure the public that it did not 'mean, of course, that the pound here in Britain, in your pocket or purse or in your bank, has been devalued', it was impossible to disguise that the UK economy was experiencing difficulties.[6]

Devaluation was ultimately a response to the UK's gradual loss of market share in manufacturing exports, and the whittling away of the productivity advantage that it enjoyed over its major rivals. In 1950, the UK was still an industrial powerhouse, responsible for almost a quarter of the world's manufacturing exports. Some 40% of UK workers were in manufacturing jobs, and they were significantly more productive than the workforce in France and Germany. The UK built more cars than any other nation in Europe. Over the subsequent two decades, however, this share of the export market declined inexorably, and many other nations not only caught up with, but even surpassed, the UK's productivity rates.[7] By the early 1970s, anxieties about the UK's apparent decline reached near panic levels in some circles. Fingers were pointed in many directions in the search for culprits and causes. For some, the prime suspect was the central state: it was accused of being distracted by short-term political considerations and hamstrung by a lack of expertise, which left it creating ineffective economic plans that fruitlessly sought to work against the unstoppable force of the market. Others blamed the obstructionism and greed of the trade unions; the complacency and risk aversion of management; or the poor skills and training of the UK workforce, let down by the undervaluing of vocational and technical education.

None of these accusations were without some substance, but, in many respects, the 'declinist' rhetoric was another product of UK exceptionalism – the belief that the UK, having been an industrial pioneer and economic superpower, should expect to remain one. (It mirrored the recriminations when England disappointed at major sporting events.) But it was never likely that the UK would be able to maintain such a high share of global manufacturing exports, or that it would continue to enjoy significant advantages in productivity. Countries that industrialized later than the UK could benefit from advances in technology and industrial processes, and although the devastating destruction of the Second World War inevitably brought significant short-term economic disruptions to economic rivals such as Germany and Japan, their huge post-war investments in national infrastructure, and the associated programmes of business renewal and re-equipment, often left them better equipped and more productive than UK industries. It was similarly inevitable that economic development across Asia, Latin America, and Africa, notably with the rise of export-oriented manufacturing in Taiwan, South Korea, Singapore, and India, would create a more competitive economic environment in which some higher-wage nations, including the UK, would struggle to compete in certain areas. None of this is to say that there weren't avoidable industrial and business failures in the UK. There were sectors – the car industry is a good example – where ineffectual management, dysfunctional industrial relations, underinvestment in machinery, information technology, and training led to a precipitous decline. As David Edgerton has argued, however, expansive critiques that indict the anti-industrialism of British culture and education, the amateurism of the political elites, and the lack of innovation in the state do not square with the continued strength of the military and scientific establishments, or the successes of sectors such as pharmaceuticals and arms manufacturing (where the sale of Lightning fighter jets to Saudi Arabia in the 1960s was an early sign of the rise of what would become a significant and controversial element of the UK economy).[8] If the 'declinist' theories of the 1970s do not stand up to scrutiny now, however, they were very persuasive to many at the time, and they played a significant part in the constellation of events that led to the rise of Margaret Thatcher and the restructuring of the UK economy.

## 1970s Crisis

In the 1970s, anxieties about British decline intersected with, and reinforced, two other destabilizing developments. The first was a growing sense that Keynesian demand management techniques were no longer working as effectively as they had since 1945, or that they could no longer mask the underlying weaknesses of the British economy. Keeping down unemployment rates had been at the heart of post-war economic policy, but in the late 1960s the number of people registered unemployed climbed above 500,000, and continued to rise, briefly reaching the symbolic figure of 1 million in January 1972. Many of the industrial sectors that had been reinvigorated during and after the war – coal, shipbuilding, textiles – were falling into a spiral of decline. Between 1955 and 1975, for example, the number of collieries declined from 850 to 241, with a reduction of the workforce from almost 700,000 people to around 250,000.[9] Many of the major shipyards of the Tyne, Wear, Clyde, and Mersey closed or severely reduced their capacity. At the same time, inflation was also becoming an increasing problem, rising above 6% in 1970 and continuing on an upward trajectory. This combination caused increasing tensions between management and workers in many sectors, leading most notably to a high-profile miners' strike in January 1972 as the National Union of Mineworkers (NUM) sought to defend wage levels while prices rose and pits were closed down.

There was also an intellectual counter-attack against Keynesianism. There had long been voices warning that an over-mighty state would have a distorting and deadening impact on the economy – the Austrian-British economist Friedrich Hayek's 1944 book *The Road to Serfdom* made these arguments even as plans were being made for state-led reconstruction – but in the early 1970s they become more widespread and influential. Milton Friedman, an American economist who was at the forefront of the Hayek-inspired Chicago school of economics, gained increasing attention, including on the Conservative right, for his monetarist ideas advocating strict control over the money supply, deregulation, and privatization. Symbolic of the shifting tide away from Keynesianism was the awarding of the 1974 Nobel Prize for economics to Hayek; Friedman received the award two years later.

These intellectual shifts were dramatically reinforced by turbulence in the global economy. The favourable economic conditions that had underpinned the post-war boom started to falter in the early 1970s. In August 1971, the United States ended the convertibility of the dollar into gold, thereby dismantling the system of international monetary management, designed to avoid the volatility of the 1930s, that had been in place since the Bretton Woods agreement of 1944. In this more uncertain environment, the Arab–Israeli war of October 1973 triggered a major crisis. As a means of putting pressure on Israel and its Western allies, the Organization of Petroleum Exporting Countries (OPEC) cut oil supplies and instituted an embargo on the United States. Prices quadrupled, creating an inflationary shock that was felt across the world and destabilized increasingly oil-reliant Western economies. Stock markets crashed, and the global economy went into its first serious recession since the Second World War.

Anxieties about long-term decline, the loss of faith in Keynesianism, and the global economic downturn intersected to create a moment of profound crisis in the mid-1970s that would ultimately pave the way for the significant policy changes in the 1980s. Rising oil prices reinforced the position of the miners, who went on strike again to resist efforts to cap their wage increases. Edward Heath's Conservative government declared a state of emergency, introduced a three-day week, and called an election for February 1974 on the issue of 'Who Governs Britain?' Heath argued that the government could not afford to be held to ransom by the trade unions when it was seeking to manage soaring inflation and falling output, but his authority had been undermined by the poor economic figures and the disruptions to everyday life caused by power cuts and work stoppages. Labour won a narrow victory, winning 301 seats to the Conservatives' 297, and Wilson returned to power promising a better relationship with the unions.

Although the new government was able to resolve the miners' strike and end the three-day week, there were no simple solutions to the deeper economic problems facing the UK. In August 1975, inflation reached the startling rate of 27%, and unemployment was rising once more, climbing above 1 million in January 1976. The budget deficit seemed to be spiralling out of control, and intense currency speculation saw the pound fall, in March 1976, to below $2 for the first time. The policy levers that had been used since the war no longer seemed to work, and more drastic measures were required. At this moment, Wilson, suffering from ill health, stepped down, and James Callaghan was elected by the party as Labour leader and prime minister. Callaghan was a hugely experienced politician, having served as chancellor, home secretary, and foreign secretary, but the task ahead was daunting.

In his first address as leader to the Labour Party conference in September 1976, Callaghan accepted that the UK faced the 'most dangerous crisis since the war', with 'an ever-narrowing industrial base and a level of economic performance which had been in steady decline, compared with our major competitors, for almost a generation'. He suggested that the nation had 'lived for too long on borrowed time, borrowed money, borrowed ideas', and had 'postponed facing up to fundamental choices and fundamental changes in our society and in our economy'. He then served notice that traditional Keynesian responses were insufficient and that his government would have to explore different policies:

We used to think that you could spend your way out of a recession, and increase employment by cutting taxes and boosting Government spending. I tell you in all candour that that option no longer exists, and that in so far as it ever did exist, it only worked on each occasion since the war by injecting a bigger dose of inflation into the economy, followed by a higher level of unemployment as the next step.[10]

The following day, Chancellor Denis Healey announced that he would be approaching the IMF for a substantial loan to stabilize government finances. The conditions agreed for the $3.9 billion cash injection required significant public expenditure cuts and the sale of government shares in British Petroleum (BP). It was also a powerful symbol of the UK's decline: the former economic superpower had 'gone bust', and was forced to go 'cap in hand' to international markets.

In retrospect, the crisis of 1976 was less severe than it seemed at the time. Revised Treasury data later showed that the deficit was not as significant as had been thought, and the loan was soon repaid. Inflation started to fall and in 1977 the economy grew by a respectable 2.5%.[11] More significantly in the long term, the UK's energy position was slowly being transformed. In the late 1960s, oil had been discovered in the UK's North Sea, and it started coming ashore in 1975, at a time when prices were rocketing. By the 1980s, the UK had become a net exporter of oil, with immediate economic benefits to the exchequer: in 1984–5 no less than 7% of government revenues came from taxes on oil and gas.[12]

Little of this was evident to contemporaries, however, and the Callaghan government's determination to control inflation by keeping pay down eventually led to significant industrial relations problems in what a hostile press dubbed the 'Winter of Discontent' in 1978–9. As strikes spread from Ford workers and lorry drivers to the public sector, the everyday disruption of the mid-1970s returned, and was amplified by tabloid newspapers increasingly receptive to policies being expounded by the Conservative opposition. Margaret Thatcher, who succeeded Edward Heath as Conservative leader in 1975, unequivocally accepted the intellectual critiques of Keynesianism and made clear her determination to put the UK economy on a new path. After the turbulence of the previous decade, significant sections of the UK public were willing to try this fresh prescription, and Thatcher rose to office with a forty-three-seat overall majority in the May 1979 election. If the post-war economic policy framework had been reshaped in 1976, it was now ripped up and discarded.

## Thatcherism

Margaret Thatcher became the embodiment of an economic vision that sought to 'roll back the frontiers of the state', incentivize entrepreneurialism and individual property ownership, reduce the power of the trade unions, and keep down inflation by controlling the money supply. This vision has been given different labels – neoliberalism, monetarism, the new right, Thatcherism – but it was never a single, pure, or static set of ideas, and it was always interpreted flexibly in power. Many in Thatcher's inner circle, including Keith Joseph, a key ally in the 1970s, and Alfred Sherman, the founder of the Centre for Policy Studies think tank, were heavily influenced by the writings of Hayek, Friedman, and other 'Chicago school' economists. For Thatcher and many others, however, the new policy direction was about far more than adherence to a set of abstract ideas. It was based on an interpretation of the past that connected the UK's former glories to a culture that fostered individualism, self-reliance, and hard work, and explained recent decline in terms of the weakening of those values through the actions of an interventionist state and self-seeking behaviour of collectivities such as trade unions and local authorities. Different historical examples were used. Thatcher sometimes celebrated 'Victorian values', and at others spoke of the influence on her of seeing her shop-owner father, Alfred, at work in 1930s Grantham; she admired the 'Puritan work ethic', and would also invoke the teachings of 'traditional Christianity' or the wisdom of the ordinary housewife. As the historian Raphael Samuel noted, 'She presented herself as a conviction politician, standing up for old-fashioned values where others were apologetic or shamefaced.'[13] In this way, Thatcher was to transmute complex, and often highly controversial, economic policies into the language of common sense, and to situate them firmly within the mainstream of the UK's historical development, even when they marked a stark break with the recent past.

The initial focus of Thatcher's government was on reducing inflation, rebalancing the taxation system, and creating new incentives for property ownership and entrepreneurship. Monetarist targets, instituted through the 'Medium-Term Economic Strategy', sought to impose a more rigorous control over the money supply, and made clear that the battle against inflation was a higher priority than that against unemployment. The 1979 budget reduced the top rate of income tax from 83% to 60%, and the basic rate from 33% to 30%, while increasing VAT from 8% to 15%. High earners, it was argued, should be encouraged to generate wealth for themselves because it would benefit the whole economy. The interests of finance were boosted by the abolition of controls on currency exchanges and the relaxation of restrictions on bank lending. The 1980 Housing Act gave council tenants with three years' residence the right to buy their houses at a discount of a third to a half of the market value. Home-ownership was central to Thatcherism. Investing in a property was believed to encourage personal responsibility, family stability, and the consumerist ethos that fired popular capitalism; not uncoincidentally, these were values that would also reinforce Conservative support. While funding for local authority housing declined dramatically over the 1980s, tax relief on mortgages rose from £1.6 million to £5.5 million in the decade after 1979 as house prices rose.[14] All of these initial policies pointed in the same direction. Greater opportunities were being created for those with capital, skills, and the good fortune to be in the right place at the right time. Others were expected to strive to keep up.

These policies were enacted amidst considerable economic turbulence which severely weakened the industrial and manufacturing sectors. The Iranian Revolution of 1979 destabilized global markets by causing another spike in oil prices. Against this backdrop, the government's monetarist strategy encouraged a significant appreciation in the exchange rate of the pound, meaning that exported goods became increasingly expensive, and correspondingly less competitive. The result was a savage industrial contraction. Between 1979 and 1981, manufacturing output fell by 14%, and over 1 million manufacturing jobs were lost.[15] Cities such as Sheffield, Liverpool, Swansea, Belfast, and Glasgow suffered badly as steelworks, docks, and shipbuilding factories closed. By 1981, over 2.5 million people were unemployed, in the worst recession since the 1930s. A toxic combination of urban deprivation, joblessness, racism, and aggressive policing led to rioting in Brixton (London), Toxteth (Liverpool), Handsworth (Birmingham), and Moss Side (Manchester). Despite the turbulence, and the considerable disquiet of several senior Conservatives, the government ploughed ahead, with Thatcher famously telling the party conference in October 1980 that 'The lady's not for turning'. The popularity boost brought by victory in the Falklands War in 1982, combined with Labour's divisions and the return of economic growth, allowed the government to ride the storm and emerge with an increased majority of 144 seats in the 1983 general election. There would be no backtracking now from the Thatcher experiment.

The policies implemented in Thatcher's second term reshaped the UK economy for decades to come. There were three key strands to this radical programme. The first was a reduction in the power of the trade unions. For Thatcher, the trade unions were both a political and an economic threat. Right-wing concerns about the power of the trade unions had been rising since the 1960s, and were crystallized by the miners' victories over Heath, which contributed significantly to the Conservatives' electoral defeat in 1974. At the same time, neoliberal economists argued that trade unions' restrictive practices and defence of jobs prevented the modernization, rationalization, and flexibility that successful economies required. The counter-attack was launched with the Employment Acts of 1980 and 1982, which imposed limitations on picketing and secondary action. ('Flying pickets', who moved between workplaces, had been regarded as central to the successful strikes of the 1970s.) It was only when Thatcher had been emboldened by further electoral victory, however, and the necessary preparations had been made (including the stockpiling of coal), that she felt sufficiently confident to take on the miners. The appointment in 1983 of Ian McGregor to the National Coal Board (NCB), with a brief to close 'uneconomic pits', set up a confrontation with the NUM, now led with unwavering conviction by Arthur Scargill, a key organizer of the 1972 and 1974 strikes. The refusal to accept the NCB's closure programme led to a strike being called in March 1984, which lasted almost exactly a year. The Thatcher government was determined to use all the powers at the state's disposal to defeat the action, and pickets, power plants, and pit villages were all policed with unusual abrasiveness by units drawn from across the country. The miners were eventually forced to concede, and the strike left a legacy of lasting bitterness across swathes of northern England, South Wales, and central Scotland. Within a decade, a once great industry had dwindled to near insignificance. Given the reliance in many areas on mining and related industries, pit closures were a shattering blow for local communities, and many, particularly middle-aged and older men, struggled to find alternative work. More broadly, this was a defeat of the unionized working classes and their power to resist the management-led pursuit of efficiency, automation, and cost-cutting. Thatcher was successfully tilting the economic scales in favour of owners.

The second key strand of 'high Thatcherism' was the programme of privatization that marked the entrenchment of the neoliberal belief that the private sector, because it had to respond to immediate market pressures, was more productive, efficient, and creative than state-owned enterprises. There had been some minor privatizations in Thatcher's first term, but the pace quickened considerably with the widely publicized sale of British Telecom (BT) in 1984. The shares in this well-known business were attractively priced and made accessible to small investors; they were significantly oversubscribed (over 2 million people eventually got hold of some) and generated quick profits for many. With this privatization deemed a success, other high-profile sales followed, including British Gas (1986), British Airways (1986–8), British Steel (1988), and water and electricity companies (1989–92). They all generated substantial proceeds for the UK state; whether this was a good deal for the UK public is less clear, not least because many of the utilities ended up being able to exploit near-monopoly positions as private, rather than public, companies. A wider percentage of the population became shareholders, but most people's shareholdings were small. The City, big investors, and senior management were the most obvious winners. As with the miners' strike, beyond the very real economic implications of these changes there was a significant symbolic dimension. Market principles were being embedded in society, and individuals were being treated as consumers, rather than citizens, in more aspects of their everyday life.

Intimately related to the privatization programme was the deregulation of the financial sector, which culminated in the so-called 'Big Bang' of 1986. The relaxation of rules on currency transactions and lending had attracted foreign, particularly American, banks into the City of London in the early 1980s, and the reforms that came into effect in October 1986 – ending the separation of share trading and banking, and enabling the computerization of transactions – helped London to become a global hub of financial services. If mining was the past, the increasingly high-tech and transnational world of the City, with its astronomical salaries and fast pace, seemed to be the future. This was reinforced by the regeneration of London itself, most evident in the transformation of the decaying Isle of Dogs docklands area into the gleaming offices of Canary Wharf. The centrepiece One Canada Square tower, completed in 1991, was, for a time, the UK's tallest building. London benefited significantly from the wealth generated by financial services. The trend of gradual population decline since the 1950s was reversed, and property prices started to rocket. London's magnetic pull, drawing talent from across the UK, intensified, just as the north was suffering the pain and dislocation of deindustrialization.

When Thatcher was forced from office in 1990, she defiantly celebrated the fruits of her work: economic growth, an extension of home and share ownership, fewer strikes, and a more entrepreneurial society with greater self-employment and lower rates of personal taxation. (The 1988 budget had reduced the top rate of income tax from 60% to 40%.) It was true that the crisis years of the mid-1970s now seemed a distant memory. But the economy was unbalanced and its rewards were unevenly distributed. The improvement in state finances owed much to the good fortune of North Sea oil wealth and the one-off gains of major privatizations. Deindustrialization had accelerated considerably under Thatcher, and the investment in areas affected by pit and factory closures was limited. Unemployment remained above 2 million for most of the 1980s. Inequality had increased significantly, and the UK was scarred by a widening north–south divide. Solutions may have been found to the problems of the 1970s, but not to some of the more deeply entrenched structural issues shaping the UK economy.

## *Global Britain*

The economic policy framework laid down in the 1980s outlasted both Thatcher and Conservative Party rule. The Conservatives lost their long-held reputation for economic competence due to a currency crisis on 'Black Wednesday' in September 1992, when the Bank of England was forced to sell over £15 billion of its reserves trying to support the pound in the European ERM. The ERM had been designed to encourage financial stability by controlling exchange rates within certain bands. The UK, however, had entered with sterling at an unsustainably high rate, and was forced to leave and to devalue the pound by 10%. The crisis and its aftermath were a gift to the Labour opposition, and played an important role in generating the momentum towards electoral victory in 1997. But the 'New Labour' of Tony Blair and Gordon Brown was very different from the party that had taken on Thatcher in the early 1980s, and made clear that it was not going to introduce a fundamentally new economic strategy. Blair was careful to distance himself from Labour's traditional 'tax and spend' image with a pledge not to raise income tax, and Brown's watchword as chancellor was 'prudence'. This fiscal responsibility was immediately underlined on Labour taking office in May 1997 when the government gave the Bank of England the power to set interest rates, and tasked it to aim for a low inflation rate of 2.5%. Monetary policy, in theory, would no longer be subject to short-term political manipulation. 'New Labour' believed it could end the cycle of 'boom and bust' that had characterized the UK economy since the war.

This is not to say that Blair and Brown were merely disciples of Thatcher. There was a genuine commitment to investing in a fairer society. The government imposed a windfall tax on privatized utilities to fund advice and training for young people and reduce youth unemployment. In April 1999, it introduced the UK's first statutory minimum wage and established a

Low Pay Commission to oversee its operation. Higher levels of investment in public services provided some support for deindustrializing areas of the UK, and unemployment rates gradually fell. But Blair and Brown accepted the Thatcherite commitment to a liberal, open, market-based economy. Financial markets remained lightly regulated, and increasingly high levels of immigration were welcomed as a motor of economic growth. Blair was convinced that the globalization witnessed since the end of the Cold War was a fundamental element of the modern world. 'I hear people say we have to stop and debate globalisation,' Blair told the Labour Party conference in 2005. 'You might as well debate whether autumn should follow summer.'[16] National governments could not stand in the way of the change brought by the growing integration of the global economy. If Western businesses could not compete with the cheap goods flowing from low-wage economies such as China and India, they would have to adapt by refocusing or upskilling.

Much of the confidence in this neoliberal policy framework was shattered by the financial crash of 2007–8. The rise of the global financial sector had been underpinned by greater risk-taking and growing complexity. Intricate and often opaque financial products were packaged, sold, and repackaged in an interlocking global chain. When it gradually became clear that American banks had issued too many insecure mortgages, panic rippled across the sector. It was hard to assess levels of exposure, and banks stopped lending to each other. After a run on the medium-sized UK bank Northern Rock in September 2007, the catastrophic position of many of its larger competitors emerged. The Bank of England estimated that the six biggest UK banks had potential capital losses of some £100 billion; the Royal Bank of Scotland (RBS), perhaps the most aggressive operator of all, was hours from collapse. Disaster was avoided only through huge state bailouts and bringing much of RBS and the Lloyds Banking group into public ownership – an effort that cost over £1 trillion.[17] The knock-on effects of the economic crisis lasted for a decade. Unemployment rose above 2 million, and average wages stagnated or fell. Restoring national finances was used to justify a period of 'austerity' under the new Conservative leader, David Cameron, who was able to pin much of the blame for the crisis on Labour negligence. As many commentators pointed out, however, the causes were far deeper: much of the responsibility lay with the neoliberal overconfidence in self-correcting markets and a complacent belief in the rationality of the financial sector.

In contrast to the events of the mid-1970s, the financial crisis of 2007–8 did not, in the short term, generate a significant shift in economic strategy. Although many neoliberal assumptions were challenged by the banking collapses, and a Keynesian-style investment was required to prevent a sector-wide crash, there was not a marked swing in favour of left or social democratic parties in the UK or elsewhere. If anything, the economic stagnation in the years after 2008 tended to benefit right-wing populist parties with nationalist economic strategies, but Cameron, and his chancellor from 2010 to 2015, George Osborne, continued to follow the broad contours of policy that had been laid down since 1979. When Theresa May became prime minister in 2016, there was much talk of a more interventionist policy, with chief adviser Nick Timothy eager to redefine the economic role of the state in favour of working people. May's successor, Boris Johnson, was keen on 'levelling up' areas of the country that had fallen behind. The travails of Brexit, and subsequently the Covid pandemic, so dominated the political agenda, however, that there was little space to flesh out these ideas.

As the UK entered the 2020s, one of the most striking features of the political environment was a lack of coherence about economic policy, and the absence of a uniting vision for national development. The collisions of past and future created confusion. For proponents of Brexit, like Johnson, the UK's departure from the EU and its 'restrictive' economic regime offered the opportunity for buccaneering entrepreneurs to resurrect some of the global trading relationships of the past. This was an essentially neoliberal strategy refracted around ideas about imperial history. At the same time, the Covid-19 pandemic reinforced the lessons of 2007–8 that the state was the essential and irreplaceable backstop in time of need. In 2020–1, the state ran up unprecedented debts supporting business and paying wages as economic activity dropped precipitately. Chancellor Rishi Sunak pushed up national insurance taxes to support further spending on health and social care, but let it be known to disgruntled backbenchers that he was a low-tax Conservative at heart. It was increasingly accepted that climate change would require significant state investment in green technologies to reduce carbon emissions, but how that would be funded remained uncertain, and there was a tendency to assume that difficult decisions could be handed over to future administrations. As political leaders struggled to articulate a persuasive strategy, living standards stagnated and the millennial generation stared bleakly at the prospect of being less prosperous than their parents while struggling to cope with the dangers of climate change. The post-war dream of steady, and shared, economic improvement seemed fanciful while the UK continued to be hobbled by the inequalities and imbalances bequeathed by the past.

# 3

# From Cradle to Grave

If UK citizens were fighting against Hitler's Germany in the Second World War, they were also fighting for a better future. There was a desperate desire for the bloodshed and upheaval to have a meaning, for the second global conflict in a generation to provide the opportunity for reconstruction. The most coherent expression of this powerful feeling came in the rather unlikely shape of a lengthy and highly technical report with the drily descriptive title of *Social Insurance and Allied Services*, written by William Beveridge, a 62-year-old with a varied career as a journalist, civil servant, academic, and social reformer. Beveridge had been asked, in May 1941, to chair a committee to examine the UK's system of social insurance – the collection of welfare benefits that had been introduced since the turn of the twentieth century to provide support in sickness, industrial injury, unemployment, and old age – and offer recommendations for improvement. Bitterly disappointed at being given what he regarded as a second-rank task unbefitting of his status, Beveridge strayed well beyond his brief to provide, alongside some carefully evidenced proposals for insurance reform, the vision of a better and more stable future that so many were yearning for. 'A revolutionary moment in the world's history is a time for revolutions, not for patching,' he argued:

> [The] organisation of social insurance should be treated as one part only of a comprehensive policy of social progress. Social insurance fully developed may provide income security; it is an attack upon Want. But Want is one only of five giants on the road of reconstruction and in some ways the easiest to attack. The others are Disease, Ignorance, Squalor and Idleness.[1]

Beveridge set out a system of universal insurance he thought would, if properly implemented, 'abolish want'. But he made clear that this would only work in conjunction with a concerted attack on the other social problems bedevilling the UK, and he built into his report the assumptions that postwar governments would introduce a National Health Service (NHS), maintain full employment, and provide family allowances. None of these ideas was new, and in many respects Beveridge was working along the grain of thinking among policy-makers. What he did was to crystallize a programme of reform for a wartime audience desperate to believe in a better future. His blueprint set new expectations for the relationship between the state and its citizens, and put welfare and reconstruction at the heart of UK politics. The Beveridge Report became one of the most unlikely best-sellers in UK history. With its findings reproduced across the whole spectrum of the press, an opinion poll days after publication found that 95% of the public had heard of the report, and the vast majority were in favour of its implementation.[2] The Labour Party's instant backing of its proposals was one of the main reasons behind its landslide victory in the general election of 1945.

Beveridge believed that a bold plan could be made for the future because the constraints of the past had been unshackled by the immense pressures of the conflict with Germany: 'Now, when the war is abolishing landmarks of every kind, is the opportunity for using experience in a clear field.'[3] For all his desire to look ahead, however, Beveridge, and his many supporters, did not recognize how much his proposals were shaped by assumptions from the past which would not translate indefinitely into the post-war period. In an affluent society, people would live longer, require increasingly expensive treatment, and have higher expectations. Family life would be transformed by changed ideas of gender, marriage, and divorce. In a more mobile world, levels of migration would rise significantly. Fundamental shifts in the economy would alter working patterns and see the re-emergence of unemployment.

Nor, as Beveridge implied, could the exercise of a rational social scientific mind remove the social tensions, cultural prejudices, and political contests that underpin any welfare system. The granting of benefits had long been shaped by notions of those who deserved, and did not deserve, help; about who was a true member of the nation, and who was not. These questions about who should receive support did not disappear – indeed, with a more diverse population, they only became more pressing. When economic growth stalled in the 1970s, the cost of welfare came under considerable scrutiny – just as it had done during the depths of the depression in 1931 when disagreements about cuts to unemployment benefit brought down the Labour government. Margaret Thatcher's Conservatives sought to trim the welfare state by encouraging self-reliance and attacking what she perceived to be an emerging 'dependency culture'. While there are some parallels between the trajectories of the debates about the economy, as discussed in the previous chapter, and about welfare – namely a post-war faith in state action that was gradually eroded and replaced by a belief in market-based and consumer-oriented solutions – the ultimate outcomes were significantly different. Neither Thatcher nor later sceptics like David Cameron and George Osborne were able to dismantle the welfare state. The NHS, as the Conservative politician Nigel Lawson would wryly observe, 'is the closest thing the English people have now to a religion'. Its huge symbolic resonance was clear during the Covid-19 pandemic in 2020–1, when banners supporting the NHS hung from countless windows around the country, and individuals stood on doorsteps applauding the tireless efforts of staff treating coronavirus patients. The pandemic, however, also exposed the continuing health and wellbeing inequalities across the nation. 'Want' had not been eliminated, as Beveridge had hoped. Despite the UK's riches, thousands relied on food banks and slept on the streets, while the arguments about who deserved support raged on.

## *Building a Welfare State*

At the heart of the post-war welfare system was the principle of universalism, an expression of the solidarities produced by the 'people's war'. In place of the patchwork and piecemeal provision of benefits and medical treatment that had evolved in previous decades, covering some workers but excluding many others, the state now committed to supporting all its citizens – from the 'duke to the dustman', in the memorable words of the *Daily Mirror*'s front-page story on the Beveridge Report.[4] This was clearest in the insurance scheme implemented by Attlee's Labour government, largely following Beveridge's model. From its launch in 1946, all adults were issued with national insurance numbers enabling them or their family to claim benefits 'from the cradle to the grave' – on the birth of children, when sick, injured or unemployed, at retirement, and on death. These benefits were not given as 'hand-outs', but earned through work. Beveridge was adamant that he did not approve of a 'Santa Claus' state. Employees paid contributions from their wages into the national insurance pool, and these were supplemented by payments from employers and the state (and topped up by taxation). Housewives, generally excluded in pre-war schemes, would receive benefits through their husbands' contributions, on the basis that men would not be able to carry out their paid work without their support. Benefits were higher, more comprehensive, and more inclusive than ever before, and provided considerably more security for individuals as they faced the ups and downs of the life-cycle. There was no desire to remove the incentive for citizens to work hard, or to save prudently, but the state accepted the responsibility to provide a safety net for all.

'Abolishing want' and solving the problem of poverty was, however, no easy task, especially in the difficult economic circumstances faced by Attlee's Labour government. Later accusations that the post-war welfare state diverted too many of the nation's resources away from investment in infrastructure and profitable economic activity were wide of the mark. It was, more accurately, 'an austerity product of an age of austerity'.[5] Benefits were lower than the subsistence level that Beveridge had recommended. Sickness and unemployment payments were time-limited, and as the historian Pat Thane has observed, 'UK state pensions have never provided enough to live on.'[6] There were no clear mechanisms to link payments to prices or wages. This meant that means-tested supplementary benefits, provided by the National Assistance Board, remained an important, and growing, part of the system. By insisting on flat-rate contributions for flat-rate benefits, Beveridge was tapping into the collective spirit of the war, but at the expense of producing a regressive system. Insurance contributions had to be pegged at a relatively low level, and took up a high proportion of the wages of the lower paid. Finding the right financial balance to support citizens in time of need while keeping down costs remained difficult, and over time benefits fell below levels of comparable Western European nations.

A similar contest between idealism, universalism, and financial prudence marked the creation of the NHS. After tense and complex negotiations with a sceptical British Medical Association (BMA), Aneurin Bevan, the minister of health, managed to secure agreement for the nationalization of a broad range of voluntary and private hospitals, clinics, and ancillary services. From its launch on 5 July 1948, medical provision was now free at the point of delivery for everyone, across the full range of services, from general practice and the resulting medicine prescriptions, via dental and optical care, to hospital treatment. The acute anxiety that many poorer families had traditionally suffered about whether or not they could afford the costs of going to the doctor was finally removed. Working-class women and children benefited in particular: rarely had they been covered by the limited insurance schemes, and many families prioritized the care of the male breadwinner when money was scarce. There were dramatic declines in maternal and infant mortality, and the NHS oversaw significant successes in the battle against diseases such as diphtheria and tuberculosis. The NHS became the defining symbol of the new welfare state and of post-war social progress. For Bevan, speaking on the eve of launch day in July 1948, it would give the UK 'the moral leadership of the world'. 'Before many years,' he predicted, 'we shall have people coming here as to a modern Mecca, learning from us in the twentieth century as they learned from us in the seventeenth century.'[7] If such rhetoric testified to the resilience of the belief in the UK as a great power doing great things, the NHS did indeed attract significant global interest and attention – far more so, ultimately, than Beveridge's social insurance plan.

The NHS was, however, far more expensive than had been anticipated. The optimistic belief that an initial surge of treatment would soon dissipate was quickly dispelled. The demand for prescriptions, spectacles, and dental treatment rocketed, a testament to a long-standing neglect of individual health, but, as expectations rose and medical innovations continued to be made, it did not then decline. The escalating costs concerned Bevan, who observed anxiously in 1949 that 'I shudder to think of the ceaseless cascade of medicine which is pouring down British throats at the present time.'[8] Attlee's decision in 1951 to introduce charges for prescriptions led to Bevan's resignation, and the start of ongoing, and often heated, political debate about how to restrain the NHS's costs and how best to prioritize its resources. Even with the resources it had, the NHS had to operate within considerable constraints, particularly in terms of its estate. No new hospitals were built until the late 1950s, and it was only with the Hospital Plan of 1962 that there was a coherent programme of investment in buildings and facilities for the NHS. Mental health care, in particular, remained significantly underfunded. Nor had the universalist principle been entirely maintained. In order to win over the BMA in 1948, Bevan had agreed that consultants could continue their private practice in NHS hospitals. Individuals able to pay could still jump the queues and receive quicker treatment.

The introduction of the national insurance scheme and the NHS were two parts of a broader series of reforms and investments that fleshed out the notion of a 'welfare state' and were designed to contribute to the battle against Beveridge's 'five giants'. The bomb damage wrought by war, on top of the already pressing need to improve slum areas, ensured that investment in housing was a high priority in 1945. Attlee's Labour governments oversaw the construction of over 1 million homes, mostly council houses meeting high standards, between 1945 and 1951. Even that was not enough. The Conservatives spotted an electoral weakness, and their promise to build 300,000 houses a year was a vote winner in the 1951 election. This generated a further surge of construction. The Conservatives' bold target was met in 1953 and 1954, with over a quarter of a million council houses built each year (and more than 60,000 by the private sector), the highest levels of the twentieth century.[9] Countless families were relocated into new estates where they could enjoy greater living space, indoor toilets and bathrooms, and modern amenities. There were undoubted costs in the disruption of family and community ties, but there were relatively few who wanted to return to their former lives, and the new homes were powerful manifestations of the greater affluence that seemed to be emerging in the 1950s.

The state also increased its investment in education in a bid to raise standards, improve opportunity, and produce a more skilled workforce. The Education Act of 1944 established a proper system of free secondary schooling for the first time, raised the school leaving age to 15 from 1947 (with a stated aspiration to raise it further to 16 when possible), and increased grants to universities. Children took an exam at age 11 which would determine whether they were sent to a grammar school (focused on a traditional, elite academic education), a technical school (designed to teach those with a gift for applied subjects), or a secondary modern (the rest). Despite claims of a 'parity of esteem' between these different institutions, grammar schools creamed off the best students and were inevitably highly sought-after. Few technical schools were ever established, leaving, in effect, a dual system which did little to break down existing social inequalities. While some fortunate working-class children passed the '11+' exam and prospered in the grammar schools, the selection process was stacked in favour of white, middle-class boys. By the 1960s, dissatisfaction with the unfairness of this process led to a shift to all-ability 'comprehensive' secondaries in place of the grammar–secondary modern distinction. The operation of the education system would generate considerable political controversy across the period, but for all the unevenness of provision, there was plenty of evidence by the 1960s that standards had risen considerably.

## The Limits of Welfare

The expansion of the state provision in all these areas – welfare benefits, health care, housing, education – together with full employment and rising real wages, encouraged the belief that many of the problems of the past had been conquered. If Beveridge's five giants had not been slain, they had certainly been forced into retreat. Yet while the experience of the 'average citizen' had improved, there were many, including single parents, those suffering physical or mental ill-health, and the elderly, whose ongoing difficulties often remained invisible. Social assumptions and prejudices continued to disadvantage whole sections of the population. Many women remained constrained by the operation of the welfare system and operated as unpaid and unrecognized carers. Those who did not conform to prevailing standards of sexual morality and had children out of wedlock, moreover, were treated severely.

Most harshly treated of all were people of colour, who often experienced racism and discrimination in their attempts to access state-provided support. Much of the rhetoric about welfare after 1945 had connected the reforms to the heroic service of the armed forces and UK citizens alike: the rewards of the 'people's peace' following the 'people's war'. The wartime nation was routinely portrayed in uncomplicated terms as white and ethnically uniform, and the self-congratulatory praise of an 'island nation standing alone' marginalized the considerable contribution of imperial, and other external, forces. In this context, it was easy to suggest, implicitly if not explicitly, that post-war immigrants did not have the same claim on, or did not 'deserve', the welfare support received by white UK citizens. The bitter irony that the NHS was staffed in significant numbers by people of colour was rarely recognized.

In the wake of the violent disturbances in Nottingham and Notting Hill in August 1958, widely regarded as being caused by racial tensions, commentators and politicians focused on the competition for jobs and housing, and the potential strain on welfare, even though more people were leaving than entering the UK for most of the period. The *Daily Mirror*, the UK's most widely read newspaper, argued that 'in the West Indies . . . people take far too rosy a view of the Mother Country. They have heard about the milk-and-honey Welfare State, with its golden pavements, pensions for all, and false teeth on the cheap. They have not heard enough about our problems.'[10] This language became increasingly insistent throughout the 1960s as immigration became more visible. In the 1964 general election, Conservative candidate Peter Griffiths won the constituency of Smethwick in the West Midlands after an overtly racist campaign which blamed immigration for local housing shortages. The *Daily Express*, the *Mirror*'s main rival, wrote tendentiously about schools 'where 8-in-10 are immigrants', suggesting that local authorities were pleading with the government to stop a 'flood' of immigrant children entering classrooms.[11] Robert Pitman, one of the *Express*'s lead columnists, used similarly inflammatory language, arguing in October 1966 that immigrants were 'flooding into Britain. . . . They are not fleeing from persecution like the pre-war refugees. They are simply coming (who can blame them) in search of a better life with full welfare benefits.'[12]

Most infamously of all, these rhetorical tropes underpinned leading Conservative politician Enoch Powell's 'Rivers of Blood' speech in April 1968. Powell invoked an anonymous (and quite possibly invented) old white woman in Wolverhampton who had 'lost her husband and both her sons in the war' and had, supposedly, been surrounded and abused by immigrants. For Powell, this white pensioner whose family members had made the ultimate sacrifice for their nation represented the deserving poor – but people like her were being squeezed out of their welfare rights by the demands of incomers. Britons, he claimed 'found their wives unable to obtain hospital beds in childbirth, their children unable to obtain school places, their homes and neighbourhoods changed beyond recognition, their plans and prospects for the future defeated'.[13] This speech, which received huge media attention and became a touchstone of anti-immigration sentiment, provided powerful evidence that many found it difficult to accept people of colour as deserving state support.

Such views had very real consequences in countless decisions made in schools, hospitals, benefits offices, and housing departments around the country. There is considerable evidence of people of colour being denied, or receiving lower, benefits, given poorer medical treatment, and refused council housing. Negative assumptions were made about educational abilities, and some Black and Asian schoolchildren found themselves being bussed away from their local schools to avoid concentrations of ethnic minority children.[14] Some of this generation would still be experiencing discrimination decades later. In 2018, Prime Minister Theresa May was forced to apologize after the Home Office's 'hostile environment' immigration policy led to the deportation of individuals who lacked the paperwork to demonstrate their long-term residence in the UK. The operations of the welfare state pitilessly exposed those who were, and were not, seen as being authentic and deserving members of the nation.

## *Rethinking Welfare*

What did poverty mean in an increasingly affluent society? What were acceptable minimum living standards when people's expectations were rising and average families were becoming accustomed to homes with televisions and domestic appliances? On coming to power in 1964, Harold Wilson's Labour government recognized the need to invest in the welfare state to stop those in need slipping behind in an expanding economy. It raised pensions and other welfare benefits, established a new Supplementary Benefits Commission to improve access to non-contributory benefits, and introduced earnings-related increments for sickness and unemployment, funded by additional contributions. This was a move away from the rigid flat-rate system proposed by Beveridge, and would be followed in 1978 with a state earnings-related pension scheme. Welfare policy was starting to adjust to the realities of prosperity.

For Brian Abel-Smith and Peter Townsend, academic economist and sociologist respectively, such tinkering, while welcome, was not nearly enough. In an explosive intervention in 1965, their report *The Poor and the Poorest* argued for a fundamental redefinition of poverty and revealed how many people still experienced deprivation. In the post-war world, it made no sense to define poverty in terms of the bare amount needed to survive. 'Poverty is a relative concept,' they contended, and operated by the 'principle that the minimum level of living regarded as acceptable by a society increases with rising national prosperity'.[15] By calculating the poverty line in relation to the government's basic national assistance scale, they argued that in 1960 14% of the population – some 7.4 million people, including 2 million children – were poor. Poverty was concentrated among pensioners, the disabled, and those with larger families. Many of the adults in this last category were in paid employment, demonstrating that poverty was not just an issue of the interruption of earnings, but also one of low wages. More importantly, though, Abel-Smith and Townsend's report, and the studies that followed it, enabled a more sophisticated understanding that being poor in an affluent society was about the very real, and multifarious, impacts on an individual's life chances when they were excluded from the advantages of prosperity. Decades of research have shown that growing up in deprivation damages physical and mental health, educational opportunity, earnings potential, and happiness.[16]

*The Poor and the Poorest* encouraged a 'rediscovery of poverty' after the relative complacency of much of the commentary about affluence. A number of new campaigning organizations emerged to publicize particular areas of need, including the Child Poverty Action Group (1965), the Disablement Income Group (1965), and Shelter (1966), which focused on the plight of the homeless. There was an increasing recognition of the need to hear the voices of, and give agency to, individuals in poverty. Social problems would not be solved by a stroke of the pen from policy-makers in Westminster and Whitehall. If poverty was relative, moreover, the battle against the five giants had to be recast as a fight for a more equal and fairer society. And for all the disparities of income and wealth, the general direction in the UK between 1945 and the mid-1970s was towards greater equality. Changes in taxation, full employment, and rising real wages, combined with the impact of the full suite of welfare payments and services, including the NHS, had gradually reduced the gaps between the rich and the poor. The Wilson administration of 1974 poured further investment into the welfare state, just as it had done ten years earlier, partly as a means of persuading unions to moderate their demands for pay rises. This 'social wage' would support all citizens, and in many respects represented the 'zenith' of the post-war welfare state.[17] But the balancing act between welfare investment and fiscal management became increasingly hard to pull off as prosperity stalled and unemployment rose. By 1976, Labour was forced to make cuts to balance budgets. Beveridge had based his whole system on the assumption that governments would be able to manage demand in such a way as to prevent the economic dislocation of the 1930s. As recession returned in the 1970s, therefore, searching questions were asked about the viability of the welfare state.

## *Dependency State?*

Beveridge, Bevan, and the builders of the UK's post-war welfare structures set out a vision of the future in which poverty, ill-health, and deprivation would be eradicated by an enlightened state working in partnership with its citizens. Instead of the ineffective and inconsistent interventions of the past, central expertise and rational policy-making would tackle social problems at their roots, buttressed by steady economic growth fostered by the government's prudent use of Keynesian tools. In the mid-1970s, as inflation and unemployment both rose, union militancy grew, and the government was forced to turn to the IMF for a loan, confidence in the capacity and quality of the state governance was severely shaken, and alternative readings of the past and future were offered. What if the state was doing too much to support its citizens, and the guarantees of state benefits and free health care were reducing the incentives for hard work and risk-taking? Did everyone really deserve the same support, and was the pursuit of equality the most pressing goal? Why did the UK dominate the world economy under the minimalist Victorian state, and experience a period of decline under the interventionist governments of the post-war period? Could the well-meaning creators of the welfare state have burdened the UK with an expensive and unsustainable system that set the country heading for a future of mediocrity, uniformity, and economic stagnation?

The right-wing politicians, policy-makers, and commentators who asked these questions found their champion after 1975 in the new Conservative Party leader, Margaret Thatcher. When Thatcher came to power after the 1979 general election, she was determined to alter the relationship between the state and its citizens, and thereby reduce the level of welfare spending. Rather than pursuing equality, or enabling dependency on the state, governments should target real need, and encourage individuals, as far as possible, to look after themselves and their families. The market should also be allowed to provide solutions that would be responsive to demand. In practice, this meant that insurance benefits were reduced and restricted: from 1982, their levels were pegged to prices rather than earnings, ensuring slower growth. The value of pensions in relation to average earnings declined significantly over the 1980s, leaving more of the elderly reliant on means-tested supplementary benefits. At the same time, businesses were encouraged to develop their own pension schemes, with the result that an increasing divide grew between those with and without occupational pension payments on top of their state benefits. Employers were also required to take over much of the administration and policing of sick pay. Against the backdrop of rising unemployment, various changes were made to the conditions of eligibility. Stipulations about seeking employment were toughened, and short-term, income-related unemployment payments were ended.

The 1986 Social Security Act brought further rationalization, with new payment scales applied to what was now termed income support rather than supplementary benefit, a freezing of child benefit, and the replacement of discretionary benefit payments with cash loans. The state was also gradually withdrawing from the provision of housing, with local authorities directed to sell off council homes at huge discounts while making limited reinvestment in new properties.

These policy shifts were reinforced by a toughening of political rhetoric. Attacks on 'scroungers' and 'shirkers' became common, and unfavourable parallels were drawn with earlier, more resilient, generations who drew on their own resources to survive rather than look to the state. Norman Tebbit, the abrasive employment secretary, told the Conservative Party conference in October 1981, months after serious disturbances in Brixton, Toxteth, and elsewhere, that 'I grew up in the 30s with an unemployed father. He didn't riot; he got on his bike and looked for work and he kept looking 'til he found it.'[18] 'Get on your bike' became a familiar refrain among those who believed that the unemployed of the 1980s were not trying hard enough to find work. 'We've been through a period where too many people have been given to understand that if they have a problem, it's the government's job to cope with it,' Thatcher told *Women's Own* magazine in 1987. 'They're casting their problem on society. And, as you know, there's no such thing as society. There are individual men and women, and there are families, and no government can do anything except through people, and people must look to themselves first.'[19] A conference speech in 1992 by Social Security Secretary Peter Lilley marked the high point of this brand of tough Conservatism. After promising to end the 'something for nothing society', lambasting travellers as 'spongers descending like locusts demanding benefits with menaces', and highlighting the claims of 'bogus asylum seekers', he parodied Gilbert and Sullivan's Mikado with his 'little list / Of benefit offenders who I'll soon be rooting out / And who never would be missed'. There were 'scores of other frauds to tackle', including 'young ladies who get pregnant just to jump the housing queue', 'dads who won't support the kids of the ladies they have kissed', and 'sponging socialists'.[20] The implication was that previous governments had been naïvely unaware that too much welfare support was counterproductive, and that benefits systems would be abused without rigorous control.

Thatcherite policy and rhetoric, against the backdrop of a regionally uneven economy, created a more unequal and divided nation. In stark contrast to the universalist tones of the immediate post-war period, the UK in the 1980s was fast becoming a society of winners and losers. The 'yuppies' – young upwardly mobile professionals, often in the City or running their own businesses – represented the winners, as did skilled workers who could afford to buy their council houses under the 'Right to Buy' policy and prospered as property prices rose. Those in declining industrial areas with bleak employment prospects, and those reliant on state benefits without other forms of support, were the losers, and, given the harsh language used against them, were often made to feel responsible for their own situation. One conspicuous sign of this inequality was the rise in homelessness. Official figures for those designated homeless showed a rise from 70,000 to 180,000 between 1979 and 1992, but this did not include those sleeping on the street. Shelter estimated in 1993 that there were over 8,000 people in this desperate position in 1993.[21] The journalist Nicholas Timmins was partly moved to write an awarding-winning history of the welfare state, first published in 1995, out of

> anger that it is impossible now to travel on the London underground or walk the streets of our big cities without finding beggars, or, more often, without beggars finding us. That, in my lifetime, did not happen before the late 1980s. There were the down-and-outs on the Embankment. . . . But there were no young people, their lives blighted, sleeping in doorways in the Strand.[22]

For Thatcher's supporters, these rough sleepers were regrettable casualties of a necessary political project that had resurrected the UK from the decline of the 1970s; for her opponents, they were symbols of a society that had lost its heart.

## New Labour and Beyond: The Battle for the Welfare State

For all Thatcher's impact on the welfare state, she was not able to reshape it as radically as she may have wished. Rhetoric did not always match reality, and it was not politically feasible to make the sort of cuts that some on the right proposed. Social security spending rose by 23% in real terms between 1979–80 and 1990–1, partly because unemployment remained so high.[23] The NHS, too, had to be treated carefully. 'The National Health Service is safe with us,' Thatcher told the party conference in 1982, and, as her biographer Charles Moore notes, she 'never ceased to worry that the NHS had the potential to destroy her politically and electorally'.[24] Although her administration encouraged the expansion of private health insurance, and facilitated the outsourcing of services, Thatcher rejected proposals to privatize the NHS or to impose charges for GP visits or overnight hospital stays. The culmination of her NHS reforms came with the 1990 Health Service and Community Care Act, which created a new 'internal market' within the health service, in which hospitals became independent trusts that could contract for services from different providers. The imposition of market discipline onto health care was supposed to drive efficiency and innovation, but there was no compromise with the fundamental 'free at the point of delivery' principle that had underpinned the NHS since 1948, and spending on the health service continued to rise.

Perhaps more significantly, the problems and inequalities generated by Conservative policies created significant political opportunities that Labour, under the leadership of Tony Blair and Gordon Brown from 1994, were able to exploit. Politicians and the right-wing press could generate short-term outrage about apparent cases of 'scrounging' or excessive benefit awards, but opinion polls continued to show high levels of support for welfare spending and investment in the NHS. The lengthening of hospital waiting lists, and examples of poor treatment, on top of the conspicuous gaps in prosperity between north and south, and the rise in homelessness, gave 'New Labour' plenty of scope to attack the Conservatives as uncaring and unsympathetic. On the eve of the 1997 general election, Blair claimed that there were '24 hours to save the NHS', and his promises of a fairer country with an improved welfare state were central to Labour's landslide victory. There was a widespread sense that if Thatcherite prescriptions had been relevant for the difficulties of the 1970s, the UK, looking towards the new millennium, should aspire to modernize and improve its public realm, and create a less divided nation. Theresa May, chair of the Conservative Party, admitted to the annual conference in 2002 that members had been caught on the wrong side of this shift in opinion. 'There's a lot we need to do in this party of ours. Our base is too narrow and so, occasionally, are our sympathies. You know what some people call us – the Nasty Party.'[25]

The decade after Labour's victory did indeed see considerable investment in the welfare state. There were dramatic increases in spending on the NHS as Blair pledged to raise levels to the EU average, rather than significantly below, as was the case by the 1990s. This spending was not always well targeted or efficiently managed, and hospitals built under the controversial 'private finance initiative' (PFI) often incurred high long-term borrowing costs, but there were measurable improvements in patient outcomes and satisfaction levels, staff numbers increased, and waiting times, which had been under such scrutiny, were reduced. There were also significant increases in education funding, with a new regime of testing and targets designed to raise literacy and numeracy levels. The emphasis on the unemployed seeking work did not change, but, with the much touted 'New Deal', far greater resources were provided for training and advising young people to find work. In 1999, the new statutory minimum wage was supplemented by Working Families Tax Credit, a means-tested supplement delivered via the tax system, which was designed to address poverty caused by low wages. Blair also tried to recapture some of the idealistic spirit of the mid-century reformers and restore the sheen of a tarnished vision. In a 1999 lecture commemorating Beveridge, he spoke of his desire to make the 'welfare state popular again' and to 'restore public trust and confidence' in a system that had become associated with 'fraud, abuse, laziness, a dependency culture, social irresponsibility encouraged by welfare dependency'. To make the welfare state a 'force for progress', it would need to provide 'real security and opportunity'. At the centre of this vision was a striking pledge to be 'the first generation to end child poverty for ever', with the target of 2020 for it to be eradicated.[26] This would be achieved not just through enhanced funding for health, benefits, and education, but also through a programme of community 'Sure Start' centres to support young children in deprived areas, an extension of maternity leave, government payments into child trust funds, and new Educational Maintenance Allowances (EMAs) to support people from low-income families to stay in education until they were 18. It was a bold vision of a more equal future that was understandably appealing to many voters.

New Labour's ambitious programme of investment improved the infrastructure of the welfare state and reduced levels of poverty significantly. The shift to a less divisive political rhetoric helped the less fortunate in society. But the Blair and Brown administrations were unable to realize their grander ambitions, or to reduce inequality more quickly, without more decisive interventions to rebalance the unevenness in the economy or to address the housing market, where rising prices left many priced out of buying their own home. Nor was the reinforcement of welfare idealism sufficient to preserve policies when tighter financial times returned with the crash of 2007–8. After 2010, David Cameron's Conservative–Liberal coalition reprised – if in less shrill tones – some of the Thatcherite rhetoric of 'shirkers' and 'scroungers' to justify welfare cuts in a new age of austerity. Particular suspicion was directed at the claims of 'immigrants', a concern that grew throughout the first half of the decade. Benefits were frozen and capped at the level of £23,000 a year, and reductions made for householders with extra bedrooms (the so-called 'bedroom tax'). Labour innovations such as 'Sure Start', EMAs, and child trust funds were deemed unaffordable. Attempts were made to simplify the benefits system by combining different allowances into a single 'Universal Credit' payment, but alongside problems with determining eligibility and processing claims, the levels of payment remained low. Only pensioners – disproportionately Conservative voters, cynics observed – saw their benefit levels protected against inflation. As state support contracted, the voluntary sector was forced to fill the gaps. Food banks supplying emergency provisions to the needy became a common feature of UK cities. In 2015, the Trussell Trust, the leading food bank provider, supplied over 1 million food supply parcels; five years later, this had more than doubled to 2.5 million.[27] In 2020, before Covid struck, a report produced by welfare expert Professor Sir Michael Marmot found that in the previous ten years, health gaps between wealthy and deprived areas of the UK had widened, people spent more of their lives in poor health, and improvements in life expectancy had stalled.[28] A decade of welfare austerity had severe consequences for the UK's poorer citizens.

The Covid-19 crisis exposed many of the strengths and weaknesses of the UK's welfare state. Popular admiration for the NHS reached new heights as staff battled heroically to maintain the service during extreme pressure on capacity. Boris Johnson, the prime minister, declared in heartfelt terms his love for the NHS after it treated his own serious case of Covid. The UK delivered an efficient and successful vaccination programme that compared well with others across the world. When the economy was forced to shut down, the government spent vast amounts of money supporting businesses and paying the wages of furloughed workers. But the stresses and strains experienced by the NHS, and by local authorities providing welfare support, would not have been so severe without the lack of investment in the previous decade. The UK had fewer hospital beds and fewer GPs per head of the population than comparable countries across Europe. Covid-19 also mercilessly exposed the health inequalities in the UK population, with the worse medical outcomes of low-income individuals and people of colour an acute reminder of the legacies of the past. The economic divisions that opened up in the 1980s were not reduced in subsequent decades, and in some respects they had widened. Beveridge's bold dreams of slaying the five giants had not been fulfilled.

# 4
# A Disunited Kingdom?

All nations rely on stories of a shared past, and visions of a united future, to legitimate their continued existence. This is particularly important for states, like the UK, made up of different countries or regions with strong identities of their own. Why are England, Scotland, Wales, and Northern Ireland 'better together' than separate?[1] History shows why – just look at what the nations have achieved! Advocates of union have used history to naturalize the coming together, and subsequent rise, of a set of islands off the north-west coast of Europe. This usual narrative is of expanding monarchical power, the spread of Protestantism, the growth of trading relationships, and the acquisition of overseas territories which gradually created an interconnected political and economic system centred on London, underpinned by a common language and shared values and beliefs. These constitutional arrangements enabled the UK, by the mid-nineteenth century, to become the world's leading economic and imperial power. The empire was a project that drew in people from across the four nations, and the UK's industrial might was also well distributed, from the textile factories of Dundee, via the mines of South Wales, to the shipbuilding yards of Belfast. The epic struggles of the First and Second World Wars were powerful shared experiences that saw the state direct and draw upon the UK's resources as never before. Victory seemed to testify to the strength of the union. Against this backdrop, the obvious question was: why tinker with a successful formula? Unionists argued that if these mutually beneficial relationships were to be sustained, the future would be as glorious as the past. Division, by contrast, would lead to disruption and decline.

The persuasiveness of these arguments was intimately connected to the continued success and prosperity of the UK itself. They had always been unconvincing in Ireland, where rates of economic growth had tended to be much lower, and the Catholic majority felt distanced from the 'British' triumphs of the Protestant monarchy and empire. Ireland did not easily fit into the conventional heroic narratives – hence the rhetorical focus on Britain rather than the UK – and the union could not contain the political, social, and cultural tensions that fostered discontent among much of the Irish population. The dramatic eruptions of the 1916 Easter Rising and its aftermath left London unable to preserve the union, and the bulk of Ireland seceded from the UK in the Anglo-Irish Treaty of 1921. After 1945, these celebratory narratives became harder to sustain elsewhere, too. Decolonization, and the gradual acceptance that the UK could not match the military and economic might of the United States and the Soviet Union, eroded the confidence of those extolling the unique greatness of the union and its constitutional arrangements. In a world where nations were throwing off distant rule and claiming their right to self-determination, the relationships of Scotland, Wales, and Northern Ireland to England and its London parliament looked rather different. This was reinforced by the decline of many of the industries that had powered economic growth in the previous decades. By the 1970s, the contraction of the mining, shipbuilding, textiles, and iron and steel sectors left many areas with a bleak economic outlook. There were few sources of growth to employ the thousands laid off through deindustrialization. The policies of the Thatcher governments in the 1980s favoured the financial and service sectors based in London and the south-east, only increasing the disparities across the UK.

In this climate, alternative histories of the four nations, and radical visions for a different future, became more compelling. There was a new emphasis on England as a conquering power, seeking to dominate the UK in its own interests, and eroding the political, cultural, and linguistic differences that it faced in other nations. Parallels were drawn with colonized peoples of the empire. For nationalists, it was time to reassert the distinctiveness of Scotland, Wales, and (Northern) Ireland, and to imagine the opportunities that greater autonomy, or even independence, could bring. The Scottish National Party (SNP) and Plaid Cymru became powerful political forces in

Scotland and Wales respectively, while in Northern Ireland the Catholic minority mobilized against the Protestant hegemony that had been imposed from Belfast. By the end of the century, the momentum for change had become unstoppable. The Good Friday Agreement of 1998 established a new power-sharing assembly for Northern Ireland, and the following year saw the establishment of a Scottish parliament in Edinburgh and a Welsh Assembly in Cardiff. But these solutions did not produce the political stability that had been anticipated. In Scotland, devolution was supposed to dampen the desire for an outright break from London, but it had the opposite effect. The continued rise of the SNP forced an independence referendum in 2014, and although the status quo stayed intact, the relationship with London remained firmly on the political agenda. In Northern Ireland, the violence of 'the troubles' was significantly reduced after 1998 as the IRA and unionist paramilitaries decommissioned their weapons, and policing was reformed, but the peace was an uneasy one, and power-sharing arrangements collapsed several times. The 2016 referendum on leaving the EU further exacerbated the strains in the union. While England and Wales narrowly voted for Brexit, Northern Ireland and Scotland voted to remain. For many Scots, the overriding of a decisive majority in favour of EU membership was the clearest sign yet of the dangers of their lack of constitutional power. At the same time, wrangles over the border between Northern Ireland (exiting the

EU) and the Republic of Ireland (remaining within it) brought into stark relief the fragility of the union, and led many to predict that the momentum towards a united Ireland would become unstoppable, whatever the protestations from London.

The experience of the twentieth and early twenty-first centuries demonstrated that the UK lacked a coherent, modern, and future-facing vision. In reality, the union had relied on the exercise of power softened by prosperity and pragmatic metropolitan accommodations to local interests. In a globalized world attuned to the assertion of identity and the claiming of rights, the imbalance of resources and the unsatisfactory opaqueness of the UK's constitutional arrangements were hard to disguise. English nationalism was becoming a force in itself as powers were devolved. It was difficult to see how the status quo could survive for much longer.

## *An English Hegemony?*

All states have regional imbalances, but those between the constituent parts of the UK are stark. England comprises over 50% of the surface area of the UK, at 50,052 square miles. Scotland is the next largest, at 29,799 square miles, while Wales and Northern Ireland are significantly smaller, at 7,968 and 5,206 square miles respectively.[2] When people rather than space are counted, England's dominance is much greater. In 1951, the census recorded the UK population at 50.2 million, made up of 41.2 (81.9%) million in England, 5.1 million (10.1%) in Scotland, 2.6 million (5.2%) in Wales, and 1.4 million (2.8%) in Northern Ireland. By mid-2019, the UK's population had risen to 66.8 million, with 56.3 million (84.2%) in England, 5.5 million (8.2%) in Scotland, 3.2 million (4.8%) in Wales, and 1.9 million (2.8%) in Northern Ireland.[3] These disparities were reinforced by the location and working practices of key political, economic, and cultural institutions. The UK was more centralized in its operation than most comparable countries. The UK parliament sat in London and the capital city was very much the centre of administrative power, as well as the hub for financial services, and the location for many company headquarters. English was the language of the public sphere, and the UK media were heavily metropolitan. For much of the period, the UK's leading 'national' newspapers operated out of Fleet Street in central London, and although there were regional offices and editions, there was little disguising the predominance in the news columns of a southern English perspective. The same was true on the airwaves. That the centre of gravity of the BBC was in the south of England was unmistakable when hearing the voices of announcers and presenters on the radio and television. The clipped tones and received pronunciation that were almost ubiquitous until the 1970s very powerfully conveyed the white, metropolitan, upper-middle-class nature of the organization. Although there were separate regional programmes, an official report on the BBC in 1949 singled out the broadcaster's London-centricity for criticism; this would be a familiar refrain in decades to come. Perhaps the most powerful symbol of the imbalances across the UK was the frequent use of 'England' and 'English' as synonyms for 'Britain' and 'British' (the 'United Kingdom' was relatively uncommon usage until the 1970s). Generations of Scots, Welsh, and Irish had to put up with being silently erased in discussions of their home nation.

The dynamics of these imbalances played out differently according to the varying relationship of the smaller countries to England and the United Kingdom. Wales had been incorporated into England in the sixteenth century, and was administered from London. It had very few institutions of its own. Welsh cultural identity was generally expressed through language, culture, and religion. At the start of the twentieth century, half of the population spoke Welsh, with rates higher in northern and more rural areas. Urbanization and greater mobility, coupled with the rise of an English national media (and, from the 1920s, an Anglophone film and celebrity world centred on Hollywood) increasingly marginalized the language; by 1951, only 29% spoke Welsh. Festivals such as the annual National Eisteddfod celebrated Welsh literature, music, dance, and the visual arts, but they were swimming against a powerful cultural tide. Religion provided another powerful articulation of Welsh identity. The widespread adherence to nonconformist strands of Protestantism left a considerable section of the population alienated from the Church of England; after a long campaign, the church was disestablished in Wales in 1920. Since the late nineteenth century, some radical liberal voices – notably David Lloyd George, who served as UK prime minister from 1916 to 1922 – called for 'Home Rule' for Wales. In 1925, Plaid Genedlaethol Cymru (the Welsh National Party) was founded in Pwllheli to push for greater self-governance and for Welsh to be the national language. (After the Second World War, it reverted to the shorter name of Plaid Cymru, 'Party of Wales'.) While plenty of people in Wales felt some resentment at the high-handedness of the English, most found Plaid Cymru's nationalist ideas unrealistic and unattainable. There was not, yet, a plausible or convincing vision of future independence. After 1945, it was the Labour Party that became the dominant political force, benefiting from some of the radical political traditions that had made Wales a Liberal stronghold earlier in the century. In the 1951 general election, which saw a narrow Conservative victory overall, Labour won twenty-seven seats in Wales, against six for the Conservatives and three for the Liberals. In the same year, a minister of Welsh affairs was created, although held in combination with another post; it was not until 1964 that a secretary of state for Wales, overseeing a separate Welsh Office, was created. There was little disguising the marginality of Wales in the UK government's thinking.

Scotland had a longer history than Wales as a separate nation, and retained aspects of a distinctive institutional structure after the 1707 Treaty of Union with England. It kept its own established Presbyterian church, and had separate legal and education systems. There were small pockets of Gaelic speakers – some 5% of the population at the start of the twentieth century – but there was a much broader sense of having a recognizable cultural identity, expressed in the literature of Robert Burns and Walter Scott, the musical traditions of bagpipe and fiddle, and an appreciation of Scotland's beautiful natural landscape. At Westminster, structures were in place to govern Scotland much earlier than was the case for Wales. A secretary for Scotland was established in 1885 and upgraded to full secretary of state status in 1926. By 1939, the Scottish Office had significant administrative capacity with departments of Agriculture, Education, Health, and Home Affairs. In line with the post-war vogue for state-led planning, these were reinforced in 1962 by a Scottish Development Department and in 1973 by a Scottish Economic Planning Department.

As in Wales, late nineteenth-century debates about 'Home Rule' led after the First World War to the emergence of parties promoting separatism and self-government, including the Scottish National League (1920), the National Party for Scotland (1928), and the Scottish Party (1932). Mergers between these organizations in 1934 produced the more long-lasting SNP. The SNP won its first parliamentary seat in the Motherwell by-election of April 1945, with the successful candidate, Robert Macintyre, telling constituents that they had 'a chance to give the Government a bit of a fright about the opinion of the Scottish people', because at that time 'nobody could ever expect London to take an interest in Scottish affairs'.[4] Macintyre lost his seat in the general election three months later, however, and the SNP would not win another for over twenty years.

Scottish voters continued to believe that their interests were best served by the main Westminster parties, and, unlike in Wales, the Conservatives were a major political force. In the 1951 general election, the Conservatives and Labour obtained thirty-five seats apiece, with the sole remaining seat going to the Liberals. Four years later, indeed, the Conservatives secured a narrow thirty-six- to thirty-four-seat victory over Labour – the last Conservative overall win across the whole period. But outside the elections, there were signs of dissatisfaction with the centralized structures of UK politics. A cross-party group calling itself the 'Scottish National Assembly' in 1949 signed a covenant calling for the establishment of a Scottish parliament with tax-raising powers. Some 2 million names were eventually collected.[5] The following year, four Glasgow University students generated headlines worldwide by breaking into Westminster Abbey and stealing the 'Stone of Scone' – the traditional inaugural symbol for Scottish kings – and eventually placing it in Arbroath Abbey. A sign of Scotland's past was used to fight for a different future. These activities did not yet produce meaningful change, but they were ready to be tapped into when the broader political and economic situation altered.

The most complex series of relationships involved Northern Ireland. If the Scots and Welsh resented the casual equation of England with Britain or the UK, there was a double erasure for the inhabitants of Northern Ireland, who remained excluded in the language of Britain and Britishness as well. These erasures reflected the awkward place that Ireland has in the political and cultural history of the UK. For many observers, Ireland has been more a colony of Britain than a constituent part of a united state.[6] Evidence for this exploitative type of relationship can be found in the establishment of a Protestant hegemony in a country largely peopled by Catholics, with correspondingly unequal patterns of land ownership; the Westminster government's apparent lack of concern for the welfare of the Irish population, most notoriously during the famine of the 1840s, which led to the death of around 1 million people, and the emigration of 1 million more; and the use of the sorts of military and police violence more usually found in imperial territories, for example in the aftermath of the 1916 Easter Rising, and as London's political legitimacy eroded in 1919–20. While it is not necessarily useful to set up a stark binary between colony and metropole, it is undeniable that Ireland's experience has been very different from the rest of the UK, and that politicians in London have been prepared to sanction policies in Ireland that they would not have deemed appropriate elsewhere.

After the partition of Ireland in 1921 into the twenty-six (predominantly Catholic) counties of the Irish Free State and the six (predominantly Protestant) counties of Northern Ireland, a new and distinctive set of constitutional arrangements was created. A Northern Ireland parliament was created at Stormont in Belfast, with jurisdiction over most internal matters. At the same time, Northern Ireland continued to elect twelve representatives to the UK parliament, which retained the power to legislate on matters that had not been devolved, and usually set the policy agenda. The powers of the Crown were exercised by an appointed governor. The result was a system that entrenched the powers of the unionist Protestant elite. In the twelve elections between 1921 and 1969, the Ulster Unionist Party never won fewer than thirty-two of the fifty-two available seats; opposition nationalist and republican parties generally secured only ten to twelve (not least because constituency boundaries were manipulated to favour unionism). With limited political competition, there was little change at the top. Sir James Craig was prime minister from 1921 to 1940, and Sir Basil Brooke from 1943 to 1963, with John Andrews serving briefly between. Craig (ennobled as Viscount Craigavon) and Brooke (Viscount Brookeborough) were clear that their task was to defend the interests of Protestant Northern Ireland against the claims of its southern Catholic neighbour. 'They still boast of Southern Ireland being a Catholic State,' Craig told the Northern Irish House of Commons in April 1934. 'All I boast is that we are a Protestant Parliament and Protestant State.'[7]

The protection of Protestant interests characterized all aspects of the Northern Irish state. The Royal Ulster Constabulary (RUC) was almost exclusively Protestant in composition, and was used aggressively against Catholic and nationalist organizations. The more Catholic western areas were disfavoured in the allocation of public resources. Discrimination against Catholics was equally evident in employment and housing, and was largely ignored by the authorities. Such sectarianism was sometimes justified by the threat of violence from the south, notably in the form of the Irish Republican Army (IRA). Between 1956 and 1962, the IRA conducted a 'border campaign', striking against court, police, and military targets just inside Northern Ireland. This was presented as a 'national liberation struggle' for 'a new Ireland . . . an independent, united, democratic Irish Republic'.[8] The Northern Ireland government responded by interning hundreds of republicans without trial. The campaign petered out in the early 1960s, and by 1963 the prospects for improved relations rose with the appointment of Terence O'Neill, a liberal reformer, as prime minister. O'Neill was keen to improve relationships between Protestants and Catholics, and between north and south. How difficult this would be soon became clear.

## 'The Troubles'

A whole series of geopolitical, intellectual, and economic forces started to destabilize the UK's status quo in the 1960s. Across the globe, the right to national self-determination was increasingly asserted, pushing imperial powers into retreat and generating numerous declarations of independence across Africa and Asia. The empire had provided opportunities for self-advancement, wealth generation, and the pursuit of adventures for individuals across the UK, and, more broadly, encouraged a shared feeling of superiority against a series of external 'others'. With the empire dissolving, these opportunities were largely closed off, and the spotlight started to shine more intently on imbalances within the UK. Individuals, as well as nations, were more vigorously insisting upon their rights, and campaigning against discrimination. The civil rights movement in the United States against racial injustice inspired other social groups to mobilize, and provided a new language of protest, as well as many practical strategies. New futures were being imagined, and past events placed in new perspectives. These global shifts were occurring just as the economic growth of the post-war period was starting to falter. The Scottish, Welsh, and Northern Irish economies were less diversified than England's, and were hit harder. Mining, shipbuilding, and the textile industries were under particular pressure, with significant consequences for cities such as Belfast, Glasgow, Swansea, and Cardiff. The belief that Westminster governments were not sufficiently or equitably investing across the whole of the UK reinforced the frustrations that many were feeling about the relationship with London.

Northern Ireland, with its stark sectarian divisions, overt structural discrimination, and history of political violence, was in by far the most volatile situation. New organizations emerged to protest against the treatment of Catholic communities, and were encouraged by the reformist signals being communicated by Prime Minister O'Neill. The Campaign for Social Justice was established in 1964, and its work was then taken forward by the broader Northern Ireland Civil Rights Association (NICRA), founded in 1967. Hardline unionists, led by the Reverend Ian Paisley, were determined to defend their position against both the new movements and what they saw as potential backsliding from the O'Neill administration. Paisley founded the Ulster Constitution Defence Committee in April 1966, and loyalist paramilitary groups, including the Ulster Protestant Volunteers (UPV) and the Ulster Volunteer Force (UVF), also started to emerge. In this combustible environment, tensions began to escalate into violence. In October 1968, a NICRA march through Londonderry – Derry to Catholics – was aggressively policed by the RUC and its riot squad, the B-Specials, leading to numerous injuries. Scenes of unarmed protesters being beaten were broadcast around the UK and the world, and pushed Northern Ireland up the political agenda. But the conflict continued to intensify. In August 1969, clashes at a Protestant march in Derry led to the B-Specials raiding the Catholic 'Bogside' neighbourhood, damaging property and assaulting people until barricades were thrown up to repel the incursion. Serious violence erupted in towns and cities across Northern Ireland, leading to at least six deaths in Belfast. Harold Wilson's Labour government responded by sending in the British army to re-establish control, and to separate the warring factions in Derry and Belfast. The existing political structures in Northern Ireland lacked the authority to resolve the situation, leaving a military intervention as the only apparently feasible solution.

While troops brought some short-term calm, the military presence generated new tensions. As violence increased, the IRA, which had remained low-profile since the end of the border campaign, was re-energized, but also split by differences in aims. In December 1969, the Provisional IRA was formed, and quickly became the most active and militant wing of the organization. The 'Provos' regarded British troops as an illegitimate occupying force and were willing to use military tactics to drive them out. The British army's aggressive interventions in Catholic areas, and the introduction in August 1971 of internment without trial in an attempt to reduce IRA activities, only led to a hardening of opinion. Radicalization was occurring on the unionist side too. In 1971 Ian Paisley divided unionism by establishing the hardline Democratic Unionist Party (DUP), while the Ulster

Defence Association (UDA) was formed to bring together Protestant paramilitary groups. By the end of 1971, over 170 people had been killed in 'the troubles'. The point of no return came on 30 January 1972 when troops from the 1st Battalion, Parachute Regiment, opened fire on an unarmed civil rights march in Derry. Fourteen Catholic participants were killed in an action a later inquiry would declare as 'unjustifiable'.[9] Catholic communities were inflamed and lost any trust they had in the army's neutrality. The IRA responded by taking their bombing campaign to the English mainland. In February 1972, seven people were killed in an attack on the Parachute Regiment's base in Aldershot, the first in a long line of actions that would lead to civilian casualties across England. The following month, the Heath government suspended the Stormont assembly and imposed direct rule from Westminster. Devolved government would not return for any more than a few months until the end of the century.

There is insufficient space here to explore the twists and turns of 'the troubles' as they developed over the next two decades. This history is incomplete and remains contested, with revelations about military and paramilitary activities continuing to emerge in the present. There were various attempts to find pathways to agreement. In March 1973, the UK's first referendum was held as Northern Ireland's electors were asked whether they wanted to remain part of the UK. The answer was almost unanimously

'Yes', at 98.9% of the vote. Turnout was low, however (58.6%), and Catholic communities largely boycotted the poll, which failed to 'take the border out of politics' as the government had hoped.[10] The Sunningdale Agreement of December 1973 established a power-sharing executive, but it collapsed the following May. Another attempt in 1982 met a similar fate. In November 1985, Margaret Thatcher and the Irish Taoiseach (prime minister) Garret FitzGerald signed the Anglo-Irish agreement to affirm that 'any change in the status of Northern Ireland would only come about with the consent of the majority of people in Northern Ireland', while also producing mechanisms for discussions between London and Dublin about relevant issues. Although a step forward, it did not lay the basis for substantial movement in Belfast. Constructive engagement was made all but impossible by the continued violence on both sides. In mainland Britain, ongoing attacks left majority public opinion hostile to concessions to nationalists. In 1974, twenty-six people were killed by IRA bombs in pubs in Guildford and Birmingham, while 1979 witnessed the assassinations of Airey Neave MP, one of Margaret Thatcher's closest confidants, by the Irish National Liberation Army (INLA) and Lord Mountbatten, the Queen's cousin, by the IRA. In October 1984, the IRA attacked the Grand Hotel in Brighton during the Conservative Party conference, killing five people and narrowly missing Thatcher herself. The IRA, conversely, pointed to what it regarded as the suspension of due process in the introduction of 'Diplock Courts' to try those allegedly involved in paramilitary activity without juries, and in denying political status to those imprisoned. In March 1981, IRA member Bobby Sands died in a hunger strike against conditions in the Maze prison; nine other republican prisoners would follow suit. On both sides, every action and counter-action was interpreted from the perspective of deeply entrenched historical narratives about the legitimacy or otherwise of the UK's involvement in Ireland; significant numbers were prepared to commit violence, and kill, in service of their vision of a desired future. Between 1969 and 1998, over 3,500 people lost their lives as a result.

## Scottish and Welsh Nationalism

Developments in Scotland and Wales were far less dramatic than in Northern Ireland, but the conspicuous rise of nationalism in both countries from the mid-1960s reinforced the growing belief that the constitutional structures of the UK were outdated and needed reform. In Wales, language remained central to nationalist thinking. The Welsh Language Society, founded in 1963, channelled the contemporary spirit of protest and carried out sit-ins and demonstrations against government and local authority buildings that did not provide information in Welsh. Activists graffitied and obscured English road signs. The flooding in 1965 of the village of Capel Celyn, near Bala in

Gwynedd, to create a reservoir to serve the Liverpool area caused widespread anger in Wales, but the united opposition of Welsh MPs at Westminster failed to overturn the decision. In Scotland, the siting of the Polaris submarine, Britain's nuclear deterrent, at the Holy Loch base in Argyll from 1961 stirred the opposition of peace campaigners and nationalists alike. At a stroke, the government in London had put Scotland on the front line of a potential Cold War nuclear confrontation. At the same time, the increasing difficulties of the Clyde shipbuilders in Glasgow – Fairfields, one of the leading firms, went bust in 1965 – intensified concerns about the future of Scottish industry.

In both Wales and Scotland, nationalist electoral breakthroughs helped to publicize these discontents and move them up the political agenda in Westminster. In July 1966, Gwynfor Evans became Plaid Cymru's first MP after unexpectedly defeating Labour in the Carmarthen by-election. Large Labour majorities were threatened in further by-elections in Rhondda West (1967) and Caerphilly (1968). In November 1967, meanwhile, Winifred Ewing won the Hamilton by-election to give the SNP its first seat since 1945. This shock victory came months after a good SNP showing in the Glasgow Pollok by-election. These striking results, coming so close together in different places, could not be ignored. In 1967, the Wilson government passed a Welsh Language Act which removed restrictions on the use of Welsh in official proceedings and documentation. Spotting an opportunity for electoral advantage, Conservative leader Edward Heath in May 1968 proposed a directly elected Scottish Assembly. The government responded by establishing a Royal Commission on the Constitution (chaired by Lord Kilbrandon). There was a growing belief that the status quo was unlikely to hold.

The economic downturn of the 1970s did no favours to the unionist cause. Inflation and job losses could be blamed on failures, or a lack of attention, in London. The discovery of oil in the Forties field in the North Sea further changed the dynamics of these debates. The SNP adopted the potent slogan 'It's Scotland's Oil', and the logic of benefiting from the riches of 'black gold' seemed compelling to many Scots witnessing the structural decline of several major industries. After winning one seat at the 1970 general election, the SNP surged to seven seats in February 1974, and to eleven in October 1974, with over 30% of the Scottish vote. Plaid Cymru won three seats in October 1974, overtaking the Liberals in Wales. The momentum was now very much in favour of devolution. In 1973, the Kilbrandon Commission recommended directly elected assemblies for Scotland and Wales, and by 1976 the Wilson government had introduced legislation to bring these into being. The proposals remained highly controversial, and over the next two years a considerable amount of parliamentary time was expended debating them, with bills failing and having to be reintroduced. Before the legislation was approved, an amendment was carried – against the government – requiring that a minimum of 40% of each electorate vote 'Yes' to devolution for it to be enacted. This proved to be a fateful decision. In polls held on 1 March 1979, 33% of Scots voted 'Yes', 31% 'No', and 36% did not vote, while in Wales, only 12% voted 'Yes', with 47% voting 'No' and another 41% not voting at all. This was a disaster for campaigners. Devolution was now off the agenda for the foreseeable future, and the momentum that had been generated over the previous decade had been lost. Although economic dislocation and turbulence at Westminster had weakened the authority of London rule, it had also damaged the credibility of political institutions more broadly. Too few electors in Scotland and Wales had been convinced that new assemblies and more politicians would make a difference to their everyday lives. The SNP and Plaid Cymru were both reduced to two seats in the 1979 general election; the SNP would not match its October 1974 high-point for another forty years.

If the 1970s proved to be a false dawn, the structural forces weakening the UK's constitutional arrangements remained in place. For many in Wales and Scotland, indeed, the 1980s proved to be a bitter period that demonstrated exactly why power needed to be dispersed. Margaret Thatcher's government showed little inclination to support declining industries and seemed to have few solutions to the rising unemployment that was scarring cities such as Glasgow and Swansea. Its harsh treatment of the miners in the strike of 1984–5 irredeemably alienated many working-class communities, especially against the backdrop of economic policies that seemed to favour the City of London and the south-east. The choice of Scotland to pilot the widely disliked 'poll tax' – which financed local authorities through a charge on individuals, rather than properties – was another provocative move that generated considerable discontent. These experiences produced a dramatic collapse in support for Conservatism. In the May 1979 general election, the Conservative Party won twenty-two seats in Scotland and eleven in Wales. This was, in both cases, exactly half of the Labour total, but still well ahead of any rivals. By 1992, these totals had dropped to eleven in Scotland and six in Wales, and then, in 1997, came the ultimate humiliation: no seats gained in either country. The Conservatives had shrunk to an English party, and UK politics was more starkly divided by nation than ever before.

## *New Constitutional Settlement*

Tony Blair's New Labour government swept to power promising to update the UK's constitution and bring elected assemblies to Scotland and Wales. Devolution fitted Blair's strategic purposes very well. It matched his modernizing rhetoric, marked a break from Thatcherism, and seemed likely to reinforce Labour support in both countries. Referendums were speedily organized and, with activists enthusiastically mobilizing to avoid a repeat of 1979, the Scottish and Welsh publics endorsed the policy. In Scotland, the result was emphatic, with 74.3% voting for a Scottish parliament, on a turnout of 60%, and 63.5% agreeing that it should have tax-raising powers. The vote in favour of a Welsh Assembly – with fewer powers than in Scotland – was far tighter: 50.3% in favour on a turnout of 50.1%. Elections followed in May 1999, with Labour becoming the dominant party in both bodies, and the SNP and Plaid Cymru comfortably beating the Conservatives into second place. The use of proportional representation was designed to even out some of the anomalies of Westminster's first-past-the-post system, and also brought the election of a higher proportion of female members. In 2002, 52% of the members elected to the Welsh Assembly were women, making it the first elected assembly in the world to achieve gender equality in its make-up.[11] The electoral systems encouraged coalition-making, with Labour–Liberal agreements a feature of early governments in both Scotland and Wales.

The devolved administrations gradually used their powers to develop policies that marked them out from England, particularly in the fields of education and health. There was a resistance to the marketization of education and the imposition of testing regimes. The Scottish government did not impose university fees for home students, and provided free social care for disabled and older people. The Welsh government introduced maintenance grants for Welsh university students, and sought to improve childcare and support for carers. Although both administrations inevitably faced some scepticism and criticism, they soon became a familiar part of the constitutional landscape. The best evidence of the success of devolution was that both governments were able to extend their remits. In a referendum in March 2011, the Welsh electorate comfortably supported an expansion of powers for the Welsh administration. The Scotland Act of 2012, meanwhile, gave the Scottish government enhanced fiscal powers. After little more than a decade, the devolved governments had not only securely entrenched their positions, they were also prepared to go on the offensive against Westminster when required.

New Labour's greatest constitutional triumph, however, was to find a way forward in Northern Ireland. Violence continued in Northern Ireland and on the British mainland into the 1990s, but there was an increasing sense of stalemate on all sides, and a yearning for peace amongst the broader Northern Irish public, who had faced two decades of death, destruction, and disruption. Secret negotiations between representatives of the UK government and Sinn Féin, the political wing of the IRA, led to the announcement in August 1994 that the IRA had agreed a 'complete cessation of military hostilities'. Unionist paramilitaries soon followed suit. The ceasefire broke down within two years, but there was a platform to build upon. An energetic new administration in London, represented as Northern Ireland secretary by the skilful negotiator Mo Mowlam, strong support from the Clinton administration in the United States, and the open-mindedness of the leaders of unionism (David Trimble) and nationalism (Gerry Adams and Martin McGuinness) provided the ingredients for a breakthrough. The 'Good Friday' Agreement of April 1998 set out plans for a power-sharing assembly, a process for the decommissioning of weapons, the early release of prisoners, a wide-ranging review of policing and the justice system, and regular ministerial conferences between North and South. Underlying it all was the acceptance that the status of Northern Ireland could only be changed with the consent of its people, and the Republic therefore formally withdrew its claim to the sovereignty of the island. In May 1998, the agreement was resoundingly approved in a referendum, with 71.1% in favour on a turnout of 81.1%. A parallel referendum in the Republic saw 94.4% of voters in favour. Assembly elections soon followed, with Ulster Unionist leader David Trimble elected first minister as leader of the largest party, and Seamus Mallon of the nationalist Social Democratic and Labour Party (SDLP) as his deputy.

The road ahead was by no means smooth, with the initial establishment of an executive delayed, and the assembly being suspended a number of times over subsequent years. Nor did violence disappear from the streets of Northern Ireland. Nevertheless, the habits of political cooperation were gradually established, leading to some highly symbolic, and previously unimaginable, moments. In 2007, Ian Paisley, for so long the fieriest and most intransigent of unionists, took up the post of first minister with Sinn Féin's Martin McGuinness, a former leader of the IRA, serving as his deputy. The two men developed a close and amiable working relationship. In 2016, Queen Elizabeth visited Northern Ireland and had a private audience with McGuinness. For republicans, the royal family had long represented the oppressive British occupying state; hence the IRA's assassination of Lord Mountbatten. The image of McGuinness and the Queen politely greeting each other was a powerful sign that pages of history had been turned, and that new futures were being imagined.

## *Recurrent Tensions*

While New Labour's constitutional restructuring can largely be deemed a success in the short term, it did not provide the stable or lasting solution that its architects had anticipated. In Scotland, especially, devolution was intended to derail the independence movement by providing a measure of local control without the risks of breaking free from the union. It was anticipated that even if the nationalist SNP entered government, it would be as a coalition partner alongside unionist partners. The SNP, however, demonstrated a political adroitness that outflanked its rivals. In 2007, Alex Salmond became first minister of an SNP minority government. Four years later, the party was re-elected with a majority, and demanded a referendum on Scottish independence. The referendum held in September 2014 maintained the status quo – 55.3% voted 'No' against 44.7% 'Yes' on an impressive turnout of 84.6% – but the margin was closer than many complacent unionists had imagined. That so many voters were not satisfied with devolution and sought independence, even with the inevitable economic and fiscal challenges that a split would involve, showed the appeal and cultural power of a modern Scottish identity that had evolved in the previous decades, and which was successfully juxtaposed against the perceived insularity and London-centricity of English elites. This was powerfully evident during general elections, when Labour saw its voting base collapse in the way the Conservatives' had two decades earlier. The forty-one Scottish seats that Labour had won in 2010 dwindled to a single seat in 2015, while the SNP secured an unprecedented fifty-six of the fifty-nine available. Although the SNP's numbers dropped to thirty-five two years later, they went back up to forty-eight in the election of 2019, with the Conservatives in a distant second place with six. The SNP, in government since 2007, and with its position renewed once again in 2021, was undeniably shaping the political landscape. A key reason for the party's ongoing success was the fall-out from the 2016 referendum on membership of the EU. Every single Scottish constituency voted 'Remain', with an emphatic 62%–38% margin overall – the most decisive of any UK nation. Despite this, London was taking Scotland out of the EU. For SNP voices, there could hardly be a better demonstration of why independence was needed, and why the verdict of 2014 would not settle the issue for 'a generation', as unionists had desired.

'Brexit' also caused serious tensions in Northern Ireland – not so much because, like Scotland, it voted 'Remain', but because a solution had to be found to the issue of its border with the Republic. The 'Good Friday' agreement precluded any form of hard border between Northern Ireland and its southern neighbour, but after Brexit this would now be a border into the EU. After fractious negotiations, Boris Johnson's government squared the circle by conceding that Northern Ireland would remain within the single market zone. There was now effectively a border in the Irish Sea, with customs checks between mainland Britain and Northern Ireland governed by the 'Northern Ireland' protocol. Unionists in Northern Ireland were furious that the region's position within the UK had been so seriously undermined. Many predicted that there would be a united Ireland within a generation.

What the Scottish referendum and the Brexit negotiations demonstrated was the absence of a coherent vision of the union in London. New Labour's devolution measures had not addressed the problem of how England fitted into the UK constitution. Against a backdrop of increasingly prominent English nationalism – evident both in Eurosceptic campaigning and in anti-SNP rhetoric at election times – the Westminster parliament agreed in 2015 to English Votes for English Laws (EVEL). This ensured that support from a majority of MPs representing English constituencies was required for the passage of legislation affecting only England. In 2021, however, EVEL was rescinded by the Johnson government. The introduction of directly elected mayors for areas such as Greater Manchester, Liverpool, Sheffield, and the West Midlands brought further measures of devolution. But constitution-making remained piecemeal and *ad hoc*. As a major Cambridge study argued in 2021, there remained a tendency in London to 'muddle through' in relationships with the rest of the UK, with an undue reliance on informal backchannels, and a failure to prioritize a proper strategy to preserve the union.[12] The differing, and often uncoordinated, responses to managing the Covid-19 pandemic brought this into sharp relief. Campaigners for an independent Scotland, or a united Ireland, had bold dreams of an alternative future that seemed increasingly attainable. In the absence of a compelling and properly fleshed-out blueprint for the future of the UK, or a constitutional convention to draw up sustainable arrangements for the sharing of powers, unionists were relying on the power of tradition and the triumphs of the past. Whether these would generate sufficient enthusiasm over the medium term remained an open question.

# 5
# People Power

Politics, in a mass democracy, is never just about constitutional arrangements, speeches in parliament, and party manifestos – it is also about campaign groups and protest meetings, the expression of opinion in popular media, and everyday conversations in homes, workplaces, and pubs. After 1945, and particularly from the 1960s, politicians at Westminster found it harder and harder to keep control of the political agenda. Party membership numbers declined significantly, and voters became more volatile. The public became less deferential to institutional authority more broadly, and had greater expectations of having a voice on issues they were interested in. The media provided new platforms for political debate and made it more difficult for governments and local authorities to disguise problems in the running of the country. Extra-parliamentary campaign groups found new ways of reaching out to people and exercising pressure on decision-makers. These movements were often hugely influential in encouraging people to imagine a different future for the UK, and to challenge practices inherited from the past. Although sometimes the aim was legislative reform or new policies from above, equally important was persuading people to embrace new ideas and alter their behaviour. This was politics at the level of the everyday. Meaningful political and social change is often the product of millions of small decisions taken by ordinary individuals – perhaps treating daughters the same as sons; being open-minded in interactions with people from different backgrounds or with different beliefs; and choosing to recycle and reuse rather than buying something new. Such change from below is inevitably slow and uneven, and it can take generations for an idea to move from being dangerously radical to widely accepted. But new ideas also create anxiety, and are always contested. Some argued that traditional ways of doing things had worked in the past and should be retained; as others started to change their behaviour, they could easily feel they were being left behind or becoming 'old-fashioned'. Conservative voices dismissed those advocating change as 'permissive', 'trendy liberals', 'politically correct', or 'woke'. By the end of the period, such debates were being described as 'culture wars'. If the invocation of two opposing tribes was invariably an unhelpful simplification, the term did at least recognize the political significance of the contests prompted by activists and campaigners. Many of the most important shifts in the UK after 1945 were rooted in them.

This chapter explores the impact of four particularly influential campaigns: feminism; advocacy for lesbian, gay, bisexual, trans, and queer (LGBTQ+) rights; anti-racist activism; and, more briefly, the environmental movement. None of these campaigns were entirely new in the post-war period, and some – notably feminism – could already point to notable successes. Nor were any of them exclusive to the UK. Radical and reformist ideas travelled around the globe, along with people, resources, and protest strategies. But we cannot understand the history of the UK since 1945 without examining the effects of these campaigns on public and private life. The position of women, LGBTQ+ individuals, and people of colour was transformed in the seventy-five years after the Second World War. Discrimination and inequality remained all too common, but popular attitudes travelled a considerable way, and social practices had in many cases been dramatically altered. Our understanding of humanity's impact on the environment was similarly reoriented. By the turn of the 2020s, few people were unaware of the damage caused by the carbon emissions from the burning of fossil fuels for energy and travel, by the industrial and agricultural release of methane, and by the plastic waste produced by our hyper-consumerist societies. The UK government, like others across the world, was committed to a strategy for carbon reduction, and recycling activities had become part of everyday life. Yet if broad swathes of the public had been persuaded across all of these campaigns, there remained considerable disagreement about what more needed to be done, and how much of a priority it should be. How far should the drive for equality go? How quickly should the UK become carbon neutral? How did the needs of the future balance with the claims of the present? Each of these movements ultimately sought far-reaching structural change, and while individuals were often persuaded of the value of incremental changes to personal behaviour, they were often more wary about more radical interventions into social practices and everyday life.

## Feminism

Feminism, in its most expansive definition of advocacy for the equal rights of women and men, has a long tradition in the UK, dating back at least to Mary Wollstonecraft's treatise *A Vindication of the Rights of Woman* in 1792. By the second half of the nineteenth century, an established, and diverse, movement had emerged. There were campaigns to open up educational and employment opportunities, to reform inequalities in the laws governing marriage and divorce, to protect women and children from sexual abuse, and, most prominently, to obtain the vote. In the first decade of the twentieth century, the 'suffragettes' of the Women's Social and Political Union (WSPU), and related groups, used direct action to push votes for women up the political agenda, although the peaceful lobbying of the National Union of Women's Suffrage Societies (NUWSS) was equally important in converting opinion. Campaigning was halted during the First World War, after which the vote was conceded (for most women over 30 in 1918, and then for all women over 21, on equal terms with men, in 1928). In 1919, Nancy Astor became the first female MP to sit in the House of Commons, and further legislation soon followed removing restrictions in professional careers, ending inequalities in the divorce process, and improving mothers' guardianship rights over their children. This phase of activity is often described as the 'first wave' of feminism, although the wave analogy unhelpfully obscures important continuities in thinking and campaigning. It also mistakes publicity for impact. As already noted, lasting change often occurs at the level of individuals, and having won the vote, many women were empowered to assert themselves in different areas of their lives. If advocacy groups did not generate the same headlines as the suffragettes, feminism certainly did not die in the middle decades of the twentieth century. There was, for example, a notable success in 1954 when campaigners pushed the Conservative government to accept the principle of equal pay for the public sector. Nevertheless, long-standing organizations such as the Six Point Group and the Fawcett Society struggled to recruit young women in significant numbers. There was a widespread belief that with the winning of the vote, the main battle had been won, and that feminism was now 'old-fashioned'.

These perceptions shifted significantly over the course of the 1960s. This was a decade in which the languages of rights, equality, and empowerment energized marginalized and oppressed groups around the world. In this context, it was no surprise that there was a resurgence of feminism. Campaigns in the United States were crucial in sparking activity in the UK. In 1963, Betty Friedan, an American magazine journalist, published *The Feminine Mystique*, a searing critique of the frustration and lack of fulfilment that many women experienced when trapped in a life of domesticity and motherhood. There was, she argued, a 'strange discrepancy between the reality of our lives and the image to which we were trying to conform' – namely the happy housewife celebrated in advertising and the popular media.[1] Friedan became the first president of the National Organization of Women, established in 1966 to campaign for equal rights. Other, often more radical, groups also emerged, many using the umbrella term 'Women's Liberation'. In 1968, a protest outside the Miss World contest in Atlantic City saw female protesters putting underwear into a 'Freedom Trash Can' in a symbolic rejection of the pressures to conform to a sexualized body image. Hostile reporters (mis)labelled this as 'bra-burning', coining a derogatory term that would be attached to feminists for decades. For all the scepticism of the male-dominated media, however, many women around the world were inspired into action.

The upsurge of feminist activism in the UK had two main sources. The first was the growing impatience of women in the labour movement about the injustices and inequalities they faced at work. In 1968, a strike of sewing machinists at Ford's Dagenham plant – whose roles had been regraded so that they were paid 15% less than their male colleagues – generated considerable publicity as the first industrial action for eighty years exclusively involving women. There were related actions at other car plants, including Vauxhall and Rolls-Royce. In 1969, a National Joint Action Campaign Committee for Women's Equal Rights was established and held a large rally in Trafalgar Square in London. These campaigns were important in pushing the Labour government to introduce the Equal Pay Act of 1970, which prohibited differentials in the pay and working conditions of men and women in the same roles.

A second source of activism came out of the counter-cultural and new left circles that were increasingly prominent in London and university cities from the mid-1960s, and often coalesced in opposition to the Vietnam war. Many women experienced a powerful disjuncture between the radical ideas being discussed in such groups and the traditional gender attitudes of the men who led them. Even in supposedly 'liberated' milieux, women were expected to remain in supporting roles, to cook, and to be sexually available. Sheila Rowbotham, a young Oxford-educated woman eager to participate in the peace movement, recalled an American activist who had witnessed her views being briskly dismissed at a Vietnam Solidarity Campaign meeting coming up to her afterwards and giving her 'a name for all these puzzling difficulties: male chauvinism'. He knew this, he said, 'because his wife, Shelley, had been in a Women's Liberation group in Boston'.[2] Rowbotham went on a similar journey to many others who were disillusioned by their treatment and channelled their radical thinking into feminism. In an influential article for the journal *New Left Review* entitled 'Women's Liberation and the New Politics', she described how women had become so accustomed to their inferior role in society, and suppressed their anger so deeply, that it was hard to overcome their reticence: 'Women have been lying low for so long that most of us cannot imagine how to get up. . . . Within us there are great gullies of bitterness, but they do not appear on the surface.'[3] Now this bitterness was being voiced, and groups rapidly sprung up to allow women to share ideas and experiences.

In 1970, 'Women's Lib' truly burst into popular consciousness in the UK. The first national Women's Liberation Movement conference was held in Ruskin College, Oxford, in February 1970, involving around 600 delegates from all over the country. The conference sought to be non-hierarchical – no leadership structure was created – and was closed to men. It issued a statement declaring that the movement wanted 'to bring women to a full awareness of the meaning of their inferior status and to devise methods to change it. . . . We want eventually to be, and to help other women to be, in charge of our own lives.' It made four initial demands: equal pay, equal education and opportunity, twenty-four-hour nursery childcare, and free contraception and abortion on demand.[4] The Oxford meeting generated energy and networks that would endure throughout the 1970s. Seven further national conferences were held, including ones in Edinburgh and Aberystwyth, alongside many local and regional meetings. Further demands were added, including legal and financial independence for all women, and the right to a self-defined sexuality. High-profile feminism was not confined to these structures, however. In October 1970, Germaine Greer, an Australian who had settled in England and taken up a lectureship at Warwick University, published *The Female Eunuch*. The book became an international bestseller, and Greer a media star, pushing feminist ideas into new territory – her work was even serialized in a popular newspaper, the *Sunday Mirror*. Greer argued that women had been castrated by a male-dominated society, and implored them to break free of the conventions and expectations imposed upon them. Women needed to lose their fear of freedom, and challenge their enemies – 'the doctors, psychiatrists, health visitors, priests, marriage counsellors, policemen, magistrates and genteel reformers, all the authoritarians and dogmatists who flock about [them] with warnings and advice'.[5] By the end of 1970, Greer and Women's Lib had put the language of 'sexism', 'patriarchy', and 'male chauvinism' into general circulation.

The central contribution of what became known as 'second-wave' feminism was to interrogate the social, cultural, and economic structures that stood in the way of equality even after political and legal rights had been won. In the 1970 general election, over fifty years since the first female MP had taken her seat, only twenty-six women were elected out of a total of 630 seats. Women remained conspicuously underrepresented in the higher professions, in senior leadership roles, in the media; at the same time, they continued to carry out the vast bulk of caring work in the home. Women's Liberation made clear that legislation was nowhere near enough. There needed to be a revolution in attitudes and a rethinking of the most basic assumptions about the family, sex, work, and public life. The widely used slogan 'the personal is political' highlighted that everyday interactions between men and women reflected power imbalances and were freighted with wider meaning. The words with which men and women were described, the games that children were encouraged to play, the allocation of tasks in the office – all of these were shaped by gendered thinking. Greer and others also pushed sex much higher up the feminist agenda, highlighting both how women's sexuality had been constrained and distorted by men, and also the extent to which women faced sexual violence and harassment as a routine feature of everyday lives. By the late 1970s, demands for the better policing of rape and sexual offences, and for women to be able to 'reclaim the night' against the fear of attack, were among the most high-profile elements of feminist campaigning, alongside the provision of refuges for survivors of domestic violence.

Feminism was always a diverse movement, and it was never likely that Women's Liberation would survive as a united ongoing structure. The final national conference was held in 1978, and divisions over priorities and tactics prevented the movement coming together in a similar way again. The most potent criticism of the feminist writing of the early 1970s was that it was not sufficiently reflective about the way it often generalized from a specific social location – usually the perspective of a white, educated, middle-class, heterosexual woman – and, in the process, could overlook, and perhaps even patronize, women from different backgrounds. Essentializing rhetoric that claimed that 'women' believed or experienced certain things could be alienating to those with different opinions or circumstances. Over time, a wider range of voices, from a greater variety of vantage points, made themselves heard, such as the Brixton Black Women's Group, formed in 1973, and the Organization of Women of Asian and African Descent, formed in 1978. This proliferation inevitably led to tensions and splits in the movement. Subsequent generations (sometimes labelled 'third'- or 'fourth'-wave feminists) sought to produce a more open, inclusive, and fluid movement that gave greater scope for self-definition, moved away from essentialism and reductive binaries, and troubled the distinctions drawn between (biological) sex and (socially constructed) gender. But judging this as a 'failure' of a 'divided' movement is misleading. It is better seen as a necessary growth and maturing of a movement that sought to reflect and represent the needs of a very diverse range of women. Most importantly, many women were never part of an organized group at all, but often still expressed an untheorized 'vernacular feminism' that manifested in a determination to be treated equally and an impatience with sexism.[6] There can be little doubt that feminist ideas had a transformative impact on the outlook and expectations of later generations of women, whether they realized it or not.

Feminism can point to numerous victories since the 1970s. A raft of legislation has sought to end discrimination and inequality, from the Sex Discrimination Acts of 1975 and 1986 to the Equality Acts of 2006 and 2010. Marital rape was outlawed by a court judgment in 1991, and the policing and prosecution of sexual violence has sought to transform ideas of consent and eradicate attitudes that left women feeling responsible for being attacked. The representation of women in the media has become much more substantial and diverse; indicative of these shifts is the Advertising Standards Authority's rule, instituted in 2019, banning harmful gender stereotyping in adverts. Two women have served as UK prime minister – Margaret Thatcher and Theresa May, even if the former explicitly rejected the label 'feminist' – as well as first minister in Scotland (Nicola Sturgeon) and Northern Ireland (Arlene Foster). Women's presence in professional roles has risen sharply; more women than men also attend university, and girls outperform boys in the vast majority of academic qualifications.

Yet equality has been extremely hard to achieve. Despite fifty years of equal pay legislation, in 2020 the Office for National Statistics calculated the gender pay gap across all employees as 15.5%.[7] The Covid-19 pandemic revealed yet again that women continue to carry out most work in the home, and the vast majority of paid and unpaid caring roles. Moreover, the revelations of the #MeToo movement highlighted the continued prevalence of sexual violence and harassment in UK and around the world. In March 2021, the murder of Sarah Everard by the Metropolitan Police officer Wayne Couzens generated a fresh wave of outrage at women's continued lack of safety in public spaces. There was similar mistreatment of women in online spaces and on social media, while the ready availability of online pornography continued to entrench ideas about women's sexual availability. There are few illusions in contemporary feminism that equality will be achieved in the future without considerable further campaigning and tireless advocacy.

## *LGBTQ+ Rights*

Advocates for what have become known as LGBTQ+ rights faced an even more difficult environment than feminists due to the long-standing legal regulation and social disapproval of sex outside heterosexual relationships (and, indeed, outside marriage). Legislation against 'sodomy' and 'buggery' – broad terms that could incorporate a range of non-procreative sex acts – dated back to the sixteenth century, and reflected Christian doctrines that went back much further still. Those convicted of the most serious offences could face the death penalty. If capital punishment was eventually abandoned in the nineteenth century, there was no easing of prosecutions, and the Criminal Law Amendment Act of 1885 actually tightened the law by explicitly making male same-sex activity short of 'buggery' illegal. 'Homosexuality', a term coined in 1869, increasingly became a category of medical scrutiny. Only men were subject to legal penalties because female same-sex activity had never been criminalized, although lesbian relationships faced similar opprobrium if they were discovered. From the late nineteenth century, there were individuals seeking sexual reform, such as the utopian socialist Edward Carpenter (1844–1929), the sexologist Havelock Ellis (1859–1939), and the criminologist George Ives (1867–1950). Carpenter and Ellis became key figures in the British Society for the Study of Sex Psychology (later renamed the British Sexological Society), which, from its foundation in 1913 to its demise in the 1940s, argued for a more scientific approach to sex. Open campaigning against the laws governing homosexuality was, however, inevitably highly constrained by the legal position.

Few men could risk their careers and livelihoods by explicitly coming out.

This situation started to change in 1954 when Churchill's Conservative government, alarmed by the visibility of street prostitution and the growing rate of prosecution for homosexual offences, established a committee to investigate the laws governing these two areas. The committee, chaired by John Wolfenden, the vice-chancellor of Reading University, recommended in 1957 that consenting adult male same-sex activity in private should be decriminalized, on the grounds that it was not the function of the law to intervene in private lives, other than to preserve public order and decency, and to protect vulnerable citizens. The current laws, it argued, failed to distinguish between adult relationships and the abuse of children, and left individuals open to blackmail. The committee recommended only a very partial reform: any public same-sex activity would remain illegal, and the age of consent was set at 21, five years higher than for heterosexual relationships. Wolfenden also made clear his personal belief that homosexuality was immoral and distasteful. Nevertheless, the publication of the report generated a high-profile public debate about whether the law should be reformed, and created a space for campaigning organizations to emerge.

In 1958, the Homosexual Law Reform Society (HLRS) was founded and played a key role in lobbying MPs to support backbench bills enacting the Wolfenden proposals. Other organizations soon emerged, including the Minorities Research Group in 1963, which was the first body to advocate for lesbian women, and which launched an influential journal, *Arena Three*; the North Western Homosexual Law Reform Committee (1964); and the Beaumont Society (1966), which sought to create a better understanding of 'transvestism'. The work of these groups contributed to a gradual shift of parliamentary opinion in favour of reform, which eventually led to the passage in July 1967 of the Sexual Offences Act, decriminalizing adult male same-sex activity along the lines recommended by Wolfenden. How little the legislation altered underlying attitudes was illustrated by the speech of Lord Arran, who had helped to pilot the bill through the House of Lords. 'Homosexuals must continue to remember that while there may be nothing bad in being a homosexual, there is certainly nothing good,' he declared. 'Let me remind them that no amount of legislation will prevent homosexuals from being the subject of dislike and derision or at best of pity.' He warned that any 'ostentatious behaviour' or 'public flaunting' might 'make the sponsors of this Bill regret what they have done'.[8] If these were the sentiments of a supporter, it is hardly surprising that many gay men were sceptical that this was a new dawn.

The desire to confront this climate of opinion lay behind the formation of the Gay Liberation Front (GLF) in October 1970 by Aubrey Walter and Bob Mellors, students at the London School of Economics.

As with Women's Liberation, events in the United States encouraged activism elsewhere. In June 1969, a heavy-handed police raid on the Stonewall Inn in Greenwich Village, New York, a key meeting place for the gay community, sparked a violent response. A Gay Liberation movement quickly emerged in the United States, and similar groups grew up around the globe. As a contributor to *Oz* magazine in January 1971 declared, 'The first task of the Gay Liberation Front is to help all gay people get back their self-respect. . . . We are gay, and we are proud of it. We want to turn all gay people on to the fact, not that "gay is all right" or "gay is permissible", but that GAY IS GOOD.'[9] The GLF drew on radical feminist thinking in its critique of the oppressiveness of gender roles and family structures, and insisted that 'gay liberation does not just mean reforms. It means a revolutionary change in our whole society.' The Gay Liberation Front Manifesto of 1971 argued that:

> Our entire society is built around the patriarchal family and its enshrinement of these masculine and feminine roles. Religion, popular morality, art, literature and sport all reinforce these stereotypes. . . . Freedom for gay people will never be permanently won until everyone is freed from sexist role-playing and the straightjacket of sexist rules about our sexuality.[10]

In its short life, the GLF generated an impressive range of activity, including the first Gay Pride march in Hyde Park, London, in July 1972, and the launch the same year of the newspaper *Gay News*. The organization itself was beset by internal tensions and did not last beyond 1973. The more moderate Campaign for Homosexual Equality (CHE), which had emerged out of the North Western Homosexual Law Reform Committee, led the way in lobbying for change. The GLF's emphasis on revolution was controversial both within and outside the movement, and some were more comfortable with the CHE's reformist approach. The GLF was also criticized for the dominance of particular interests: many lesbian women felt marginalized within the movement. But the longer-term influence of the GLF's ideas – the emphasis on an unapologetic claiming of rights, and the encouragement to 'come out' – was profound. The listings pages of *Gay News*, advertising events, networks, and venues, showed an LGBTQ+ community growing in visibility and reach across the 1970s. In 1980, the reforms of the 1967 Sexual Offences Act were extended to Scotland; Northern Ireland followed suit in 1982.

Achieving further change was difficult, however, and became even harder with the emergence in the early 1980s of Human Immunodeficiency Virus (HIV), which led to Acquired Immunodeficiency Syndrome (AIDS). For sections of the popular press, AIDS was a 'gay plague' resulting from 'promiscuous' lifestyles. The pain and loss experienced by many in the gay community were exacerbated by the hostility and suspicion directed at them by an often ill-informed public. The AIDS Coalition to Unleash Power (ACT UP), originating in New York and then spreading to London and across Europe, led attempts to disseminate knowledge and demand better treatment and support. In 1988, the Conservative government capitalized on the controversy by introducing Section 28 of the Local Government Act, which banned schools from promoting the 'acceptability of homosexuality as a pretended family relationship'. Once again, activists mobilized to resist, and Stonewall UK formed to wage the continuing battle for equality.

From the 1990s, the movement diversified and gradually found itself operating in a more conducive environment. Drawing on queer thought, a more fluid and inclusive understanding of sexuality challenged hetero–homo binaries. Bisexual, trans, and queer people gained greater visibility and established their own organizations and networks. Meanwhile, as the 1960s generation took political power, legislative reform became more realistic. Under Tony Blair's Labour government, a series of acts significantly altered the position of LGBTQ+ people. In 2000, the ban on service in the armed forces was lifted; in 2001, the age of consent was equalized at 16; in 2002, same-sex couples were granted equal rights when applying to adopt; in 2003, Section 28 was repealed and the discrimination against LGBTQ+ individuals at work was outlawed; in 2004, civil partnerships were introduced, giving same-sex couples the same rights as married couples, and the Gender Recognition Act gave trans people legal recognition in their appropriate gender (albeit with 'male' and 'female' as the only options). These changes were consolidated and reinforced by the wide-ranging Equality Acts of 2006 and 2010. Perhaps the most symbolic reform of all was the introduction by David Cameron's Coalition government of same-sex marriage from 2014. Although the legislation was hugely controversial in right-wing and Christian circles, Cameron was adamant that his Conservative Party needed to show its acceptance of equality. There could be few illusions about the continuing inequality and discrimination faced by LGBTQ+ people, and ferocious arguments continued to rage about appropriate support for trans individuals, but the shift in opinion in the three decades from Section 28 was little short of remarkable.

## Anti-Racism

People of colour standing up for their rights, as well as organizations challenging various forms of racial injustice, have a long history in the UK. In the late eighteenth century, individuals such as Olaudah Equiano, and the Sons of Africa group with which he was associated, played an important role in the campaign against the slave trade. As the numbers of black and Asian people in the UK grew in the twentieth century, formal and informal organizations and networks multiplied. The League of Coloured Peoples, established in 1931 by the Jamaican doctor Harold Moody, campaigned to improve the position of ethnic minority groups, and published an influential journal, *The Keys*. The Indian Workers' Association, founded in Coventry in 1938, represented the interests of working-class members while also fighting against UK colonial rule. Many others were inspired by anti-colonial and racial equality campaigns around the British Empire and in the United States.

After the arrival, in June 1948, of the passenger liner *Empire Windrush* carrying West Indians to Tilbury Docks in Kent, immigration began to rise up the political agenda in the UK. There was a growing consciousness of the need to support and protect the interests of growing black and Asian communities. The Colonial People's Defence Association, established in Liverpool in 1950, sought to prevent the repatriation of black seamen, and to eliminate discrimination in the workplace. Pearl and Edric Connor established the first agency to represent black authors, actors, and film-makers. Claudia Jones, a Trinidadian activist who came to London after being deported from the United States, founded the *West Indian Gazette* in March 1958 to offer a counterpoint to the white-dominated national media and brought, according to its strapline, 'All the News You Want from Here and Home'. Jones went on to play a key role in the formation of the Notting Hill Carnival to showcase the vibrant culture of the Caribbean.

The outbreak of violence between white and black youths in Nottingham and Notting Hill, London, in late August and early September 1958 – quickly labelled 'race riots' – consolidated the idea that immigration was generating social tensions. Calls to implement restrictions grew louder, even though, in this period, more people were leaving the country than entering. Media scrutiny of areas of high immigration increased, and the Institute of Race Relations, founded only months earlier, started to produce a series of sociological studies exploring issues of prejudice and discrimination, albeit often from the external perspective of a white researcher. In most black and Asian communities, there were few illusions that people could rely on the goodwill of the institutions of the state. Self-help and activism would be crucial for long-term survival. When Kelso Cochrane, a 32-year-old Antiguan, was murdered by white youths in 1959, the police were unable to bring a prosecution, despite the killers being known in local circles. Claudia Jones was at the centre of the campaign to publicize the case and to highlight the injustice that it reflected, although it remained unsolved. This example of unpunished racial violence would become depressingly familiar. A more successful example of direct action came in Bristol when four West Indian men, Roy Hackett, Owen Henry, Audley Evans, and Prince Brown, organized a boycott of the city's buses as a protest against the colour bar operated by the Bristol Omnibus Company. The boycott, launched at the end of April 1963, quickly generated strong support and considerable publicity, and eventually forced the company to back down. By September, Bristol had its first non-white bus conductors.

From the 1960s, governments of both parties pursued a dual strategy to address the perceived problem of 'race relations'. On the one hand, restrictions on immigration were imposed. The 1962 Commonwealth Immigration Act created a system requiring new entrants to possess specific skills, a guarantee of employment or study, or existing family connections. By excluding Irish immigrants, the racial dimension of the act was laid bare. Labour leader Hugh Gaitskell lambasted the 'cruel and brutal anti-colour legislation', but when Labour took power two years later, it accepted and then extended the system. Immigration restrictions would continue to tighten over coming decades, with the 1981 British Nationality Act requiring children born in the UK to have at least one parent who was a British citizen or permanent resident if they were to claim citizenship. At the same time, a series of acts outlawed racial discrimination, first in public places (1965), then extended to the spheres of employment and housing (1968). New bodies were created to monitor the success of these policies, notably the Race Relations Board (1965), the Community Relations Commission (1968), and the Commission for Racial Equality (1976).

These bodies may have signalled a growing intolerance for overt racism – witnessed in the severe criticism of Enoch Powell's notorious 'Rivers of Blood' speech in April 1968 (see Chapter 3) – but they lacked the power or resources to tackle attitudes and practices that were deeply rooted in UK culture and society. Frustrated at the limitations of official action, and inspired by more radical civil rights organizations emerging in the United States and beyond, some individuals developed a more revolutionary stance. Obi Egbuna, a Nigerian-born writer and activist who moved to the UK in 1961, co-founded the United Coloured People's Association in 1967 and published a manifesto, *Black Power in Britain*, calling for direct action against racial discrimination. He then founded the British Black Panthers, a revolutionary socialist group modelled on the US-based organization. In the summer of 1968 Egbuna was arrested for inciting violence against the police in speeches given in Hyde Park, London; by 1973, he had left the UK. Few displayed the radicalism of Egbuna or 'Michael X' (Michael de Freitas, another London-based exponent of Black Power), and the Panthers did not last; but they did speak to an anger and frustration that was more widely felt, and some of the ideas emanating from these circles, such as the need for black history in schools, became mainstream.

Over subsequent decades, progress towards equality was slow. People of colour became more visible in politics, the public sphere, and the media. The 1987 general election saw four ethnic minority MPs enter parliament, the first to do so since the Second World

War. One of them, Paul Boateng, became the first black cabinet minister in 2002. But discrimination and harassment were still entrenched across UK society, and the experience of racial violence remained common. After the horrific death of thirteen Afro-Caribbean young people in a fire at a family home in New Cross in January 1981, local black groups became incensed by the slow police investigation. They organized the Black People's Day of Action on 2 March 1982, which saw over 20,000 people march through London to present a petition to Downing Street. The Day was an important spur to black activism of all kinds, but the limited shift in police culture was evident after the racist murder of the black teenager Stephen Lawrence in April 1993. The botched investigation saw the perpetrators escape justice until a further trial in 2012. In 1999, an official report by Sir William Macpherson, a judge, deemed the Metropolitan Police to be 'institutionally racist' and demanded reform. The Macpherson Report was a key turning point. By moving the focus away from individual racist 'bad apples' to deeper structures and practices, it demonstrated how discrimination could be the result of 'unwitting prejudice, ignorance, thoughtlessness and racist stereotyping'.[11] This insight provoked many institutions and organizations to reflect on, and change, their behaviour. The Equality Acts of 2006 and 2010 further toughened the legislation around discrimination.

The response to the murder of George Floyd by the Minneapolis police officer Derek Chauvin in May

2020 showed that anger about continued inequality had not diminished. Floyd's death generated outrage across the world, often mobilizing under the slogan 'Black Lives Matter'. Anti-racism rallies were held in over 260 towns and cities across the whole of the UK, with some 210,000 people participating.[12] In Bristol, a statue of the slave trader Edward Colston was toppled. Premier League footballers routinely started to 'take the knee' before games in a sign of their opposition to racism; schools, universities, and cultural institutions were forced to reflect on how they presented the UK's history. The understanding that racism was a structural problem was more widely accepted than ever before. How these structures should be tackled, however, remained controversial.

## *The Environment*

The desire to value and protect the environment is as old as the determination to stand up for individual rights. The smoke and pollution generated by mines, cotton mills, and steel factories, the destruction of the countryside by the growth of towns and cities, the encroachment of cars into picturesque surroundings – all of these generated organized responses well before 1945. The National Trust was founded in 1895 to protect sites of 'beauty or historical interest', and the Campaign for the Preservation of Rural England (CPRE) was founded in 1926. Another strand of activism sought to stop the human mistreatment of animals and natural habitats. The Royal Society for the Prevention of Cruelty to Animals (RSPCA) dates back to 1824 (with the royal R being added in 1840), the National Anti-Vivisection Society to 1875, and the Royal Society for the Protection of Birds (RSPB) to 1889. The suffocating smog that settled on London in December 1952, leading to the death of at least 4,000 people, generated the momentum towards the Clean Air Act of 1956, requiring factories and households to convert to smokeless fuels.

The modern environmental movement emerged in the 1970s, as scientists unravelled with ever-greater precision the devastating impact of human activities. They identified, and activists quickly publicized, the disastrous consequences of the growing concentration of carbon dioxide in the atmosphere; the depletion of the ozone layer; the formation of 'acid rain' by the release of sulphur dioxide and nitrogen oxides; the damage caused by the overuse of pesticides, modern farming methods, and the proliferation of plastic waste; and the risks associated with the by-products of nuclear energy and weaponry. As with other social movements, inspiration from the United States was important. Friends of the Earth (FoE) and Greenpeace were both launched in the UK in 1971, each part of wider global networks, and became adept at attracting attention through eye-catching campaigns. Both organizations sought to persuade the public to change their behaviour while also lobbying governments for change. People, founded by Tony Whittaker in

Coventry in 1973, sought to enter the political system directly, and contested seats in the 1974 general election with its *Manifesto for a Sustainable Society*. People became the Ecology Party in 1975, and then the Green Party in 1985. By the late 1980s, the Greens were starting to create some political waves, as the public became increasingly concerned about acid rain, holes in the ozone layer, and the loss of rainforests. In the 1989 European elections – in which backing alternative candidates seemed to carry little risk – the Green Party took 15% of the vote, pushing the Liberal Democrats into a distant fourth place. Months later, Margaret Thatcher legitimated environmental concerns in an important speech to the United Nations, demonstrating that this was an issue that could reach across the political spectrum. Thatcher warned of the 'insidious danger' of 'irretrievable damage to the atmosphere, to the oceans, to earth itself'. 'It is no good squabbling over who is responsible or who should pay,' she concluded: 'We shall only succeed in dealing with the problems through a vast international, co-operative effort.'[13] Green issues were now well and truly on the political agenda.

The UK's first-past-the-post system ultimately limited the direct impact of the Green Party. Caroline Lucas became the first Green MP in 2010 by winning the Brighton Pavilion constituency, but a more substantial breakthrough remained unlikely. Scotland's proportional representation system offered a more conducive political environment, however. In the election of 2021, the separate Scottish Green Party obtained eight seats through the regional list vote, and subsequently agreed a deal with the SNP to enter government. More broadly, though, major parties, as well as public bodies and businesses, have been forced to respond to an environmental agenda that has gathered momentum through international agreements such as the Rio Climate Change Convention (1992), the Kyoto Protocol (1997), and the Paris Agreement (2015). In 2005, Gordon Brown, then chancellor of the Exchequer, commissioned the leading economist Sir Nicholas Stern to carry out a study of the review of the economics of climate change. The landmark Stern Review of 2006 identified climate change as the most serious market failure ever seen, and marked the moment from which climate change denial became increasingly unacceptable in mainstream political opinion. All parties developed extensive policies to preserve the environment. In June 2019, Theresa May's Conservative government pledged that the UK would reach net zero greenhouse gas emissions by 2050. Although the UK was the first major economy to make such a pledge, many campaigners, including the influential global activist Greta Thunberg, and the UK-based group Extinction Rebellion, argued that this action was too little, too late.

The extent of attitudinal change in the decades after 1945 was in many respects remarkable. Opinions that were commonplace became marginalized, even illegal. Politicians or public figures who questioned efforts to ensure gender, racial, and LGBTQ+ equality, or who denied climate change, were usually unable to maintain their positions. With growing public recognition of how much damage was caused by stereotypes and derogatory terms, language was policed much more carefully. Nothing made the recent past seem more remote than seeing how some of the most popular media programmes and publications of previous decades were saturated with words and images that were no longer acceptable. But equality remained frustratingly distant for all the groups discussed, and there was anger that progress was not faster. As the UK entered the 2020s, there was a much wider appreciation that inequality was maintained by structural forces, and would not be solved by good intentions alone. Reforming structures, though, was difficult and complex work, and many institutions found it easier to encourage individuals to bear the responsibility of change than to reflect thoroughly on their own practices. Climate change was likely to be the most difficult problem to solve of all. Again, individual action was hopelessly insufficient: deep economic and social reforms, coordinated across the globe, seemed to offer the only realistic solution on the scale required. Despite the urgency of discussions at the UN's Climate Change Conference in Edinburgh in November 2021, however, it was unclear that nations were working at the intensity required. In all these areas, despite very real shifts since 1945, a clear vision of how to reach the desired future remained frustratingly out of reach.

# 6
# Looking after Number 1

In July 1945, the Labour and Conservative parties faced the electorate and sought the votes needed to form the next government. For all the sound and fury of the general election campaign, there was one thing they could agree on: that there were the only two parties with any realistic chance of securing a majority in the House of Commons. Seventy-four years later, in December 2019, the same two parties fought in an electoral system that looked essentially identical, equally confident that they dominated the political landscape. To an outsider, it might seem as if nothing much had changed. As we have seen in previous chapters, however, the content and style of UK politics had altered significantly since the Second World War, with new issues emerging and priorities shifting. The reason was simple. If the parties were the same, the electorate was not. The public that politicians addressed in 1945 was predominantly white, Christian, and had a strong sense of belonging to a national community with a shared history and a common moral framework. It was conspicuously structured by class and gender. There were clear differences between those in manual occupations – some two-thirds of the workforce – and those in non-manual jobs, and men and women lived according to deeply entrenched notions of their different roles. Young people left school at 14 or 15 and went into the world of work; only a tiny percentage had the opportunity of going to university. The age of adulthood was 21, and there was little in the way of a distinctive youth culture. Politicians seeking to construct a compelling vision of the future at least faced a relatively recognizable and predictable electorate.

The nation that developed in the decades after 1945 was more pluralistic, diverse, affluent, and mobile, and, as a result, politics became more variegated and volatile. The UK stopped being a Christian country in a meaningful sense, and other faiths took on a more prominent role in public life. The state reduced its role as moral arbiter, and advanced a secular human rights regime which protected, at least in theory, individual liberty, privacy, and freedom of expression. Dramatic rises in household wealth, evident in higher levels of home ownership, the acquisition of cars, domestic appliances, and communication devices, and greater access to credit, generated new expectations. The world of employment was transformed, with a dramatic decline in manual work, and a corresponding increase in office-based and service sector jobs. The pattern of women's lives began to converge much more closely with that of men's. Young people were offered greater education and training opportunities, and more and more went to university. They wanted, and expected, a voice: the voting age was reduced to 18, and there was pressure to reduce it further to 16.

At the same time, the vast expansion of the media environment, from the rise of television to the emergence of the internet and social media, gave people access to unprecedented amounts of information and entertainment, and allowed them to participate in a broad and eclectic range of music, fashion, and sport-related subcultures. The media further accelerated the trend towards globalization. Not only did the UK become more cosmopolitan and ethnically diverse through immigration, people were exposed to global foods, cultures, and social practices in their everyday lives.

These developments have often been described as leading to the rise of 'individualism'. There is a danger here of condescension to people in earlier times – treating them as if they did not have their own personal desires and aspirations. Nor should we assume that there is any less of a yearning for community and social connection now than previously. Nevertheless, in a more affluent, mediated, pluralistic, and global society, individuals have far greater freedom to curate their own identities. They are less likely to follow tradition, to inherit beliefs, and to stay in the same place or the same occupation as their parents. People now have greater expectations of making choices about their lives and of being allowed to express themselves as they want. They have a much wider range of reference points, and are more sceptical of authority. There is a much stronger sense of being able to escape the constraints of the past, and of being able to reach a better future. The extent to which people can actually shape their own lives varies significantly, of course. It remains hard to pursue an individual path without money, education, and good health; indeed, the frustration of being 'left behind' is all the more intense in an affluent, celebrity-focused society. But even if it is not grounded in realism, many retain a strong ambition for personal growth, material prosperity, even fame and success, if not for themselves then for their children or relatives. Politicians have to navigate this terrain by creating a capacious vision of the future capable of offering opportunities for all and meeting the high, and diverse, expectations of a more individualistic society.

## *A Secular Society?*

Christianity has been woven into the lives of the people of the British Isles for centuries. It has fundamentally shaped the monarchy and the institutions of the state. The coronation oaths are overseen by the Archbishop of Canterbury and include a promise to act as 'Defender of the Faith', while twenty-six bishops sit by right in the House of Lords. The legal system was, in many respects, built on the foundation of church teaching – seen, for example, in the legislation governing marriage, divorce, abortion, homosexuality, suicide, and many other issues – and the clergy expected to have a central role in public discussions of morality. Churches have also played a major part in the provision of schooling, and the 1944 Education Act required that 'the school day in every county school and in every voluntary school shall begin with collective worship on the part of all pupils', with local authorities given the responsibility for drawing up 'an agreed syllabus of religious instruction'.[1] Many cultural and voluntary activities had a religious dimension, from scouts and guides to brass bands. The BBC from its foundation had an overtly Christian ethos and provided extensive religious programming. There were stringent restrictions on public activities on Sundays, the day of prayer, and the vast majority of shops, entertainment venues, and sports grounds remained closed.

The different nations of the UK had varied religious dynamics, although forms of Protestantism were dominant throughout. The Presbyterian Church of Scotland rejected the Church of England's hierarchical structure of archbishops and bishops, while Methodism, based on the teachings of John Wesley (1703–91), flourished in Wales. In Northern Ireland, fraternal organizations such as the Orange Order were keen to celebrate traditional Protestant teaching and ceremonial in the face of the Catholic challenge in the south. Before 1945, there were also significant Catholic and Jewish minorities, and much smaller Muslim, Hindu and Sikh communities. Even if many people in the UK were only nominal adherents to a faith, active atheism was limited, particularly in comparison to countries such as France. In 1880, the radical MP Charles Bradlaugh was unable to take his seat in the House of Commons because as an atheist he was not prepared to swear the religious oath of allegiance; it took six years to resolve the situation. Bradlaugh was unusual. In many European nations, parties of the left were often vehicles for atheist and secularist views, but this was less the case in the UK. As the Labour politician Morgan Philips wryly observed in 1953, 'The Labour Party owes more to Methodism than to Marxism.'[2]

Some sociologists have argued that secularization – the 'process by which religious thinking, practice and institutions lose social significance'[3] – is a long-term development intimately associated with industrialization, urbanization, and the rise of scientific modes of thought. The rapidly growing cities of the nineteenth century certainly provided difficult environments for some churches, while Darwin's theories of evolution and natural selection, which contradicted a literal interpretation of the Bible, led some to question the tenets of Christianity. Others could not reconcile the pain and suffering they had witnessed during the First and Second World Wars with a loving God. Despite this, the Christian churches remained strong, in terms of both membership and social and cultural authority, throughout the 1950s. Some 2 million people attended the US evangelical preacher Billy Graham's twelve-week tour in London in 1954, culminating in a 120,000-strong crowd at Wembley Stadium. Another 1.2 million saw him in Glasgow the following year.

These were audiences that only the biggest rock bands could generate in later decades. Christian teaching continued to underpin a restrictive and conservative morality. The Public Morality Council (PMC), a body representing the main Christian and Jewish denominations, wielded considerable influence over the regulation and policing of sex and erotic display in public spaces and the entertainment industry, and encouraged the judiciary, local authorities, and licensing bodies to uphold rigorous moral standards. In 1954, Donald McGill, the most famous exponent of the hand-drawn saucy seaside postcard, was successfully prosecuted and fined for obscenity.

By the end of the 1950s, however, a range of humanists, social reformers, and cultural producers attempted to loosen the tight connection between the law and Christian morality, and to create a wider sphere within which adults could make their own decisions. Reform in three related areas paved the way for the emergence of a more pluralistic society. First, as we saw in Chapter 5, the Wolfenden Report of 1957 made a significant distinction between the law and sin when recommending the decriminalization of homosexuality. It argued that it was not the 'function of the law to intervene in the private lives of citizens, or to seek to enforce any particular pattern of behaviour, further than is necessary' to preserve public order and protect people from injury or exploitation. It was entirely reasonable that some activities that were regarded as sinful, such as adultery, were not within the purview of the criminal law.[4] Although the Wolfenden recommendations were not accepted for another decade, the report generated a wide-ranging debate about the proper role of the state, and provided a potent set of arguments in favour of personal choice.

Second, there was the related campaign, led by the Society of Authors and politicians such as Roy Jenkins, to reform the legislation on obscenity. The existing law left books and other cultural products liable to prosecution if their tendency was to 'deprave and corrupt those whose minds are open to such immoral influence and into whose hands a publication of this sort might fall'. If it was plausible that a child might get hold of, and be 'corrupted by', a saucy seaside postcard, for example, then such material could be seized. Bodies such as the PMC used these provisions to insist that local authorities clamp down on 'depravity'. The revised 1959 Obscene Publications Act, introduced by Jenkins, provided a new public good defence if it could be shown that the item served 'the interests of science, literature, art, or learning, or of other objects of general concern'. There was also a tightening of the language about the likely audience. Suddenly there was an opportunity to address adults in new ways. The following year, in a high-profile trial, Penguin Books were found not guilty of obscenity for publishing D.H. Lawrence's sexually explicit novel *Lady Chatterley's Lover*, and authors and publishers rushed to test the boundaries of cultural acceptability. The third notable shift was the 1961 Suicide Act, which ensured that anyone who attempted to take their own life – deemed in Christian teaching to be a sinful contravention of God's will – would no longer face prosecution. This reflected a transition away from a religious framing of the problem of suicide and depression towards a more therapeutic approach. In all three areas, there was an acceptance that it was legitimate to hold differing views on moral questions, and that it was not appropriate to limit adult freedoms to the narrow confines of traditional Christian morality.

These rather cautious salvos against the edifice of church power soon turned into a full-blooded assault. During the 1960s, Christian teaching on all aspects of morality was questioned, and the churches' political, social, and cultural roles were thoroughly critiqued by satirists, student radicals, and countercultural commentators. Perhaps most damaging of all, Christianity was made to seem irrelevant and old-fashioned by a powerful emerging youth culture that prized sexual expression and consumer pleasure above more traditional values. Fierce debates emerged within the Protestant churches between modernizers such as John Robinson, who supported more liberal interpretations of Christian teaching and encouraged a rethinking of the conventional understandings of God, and traditionalists and evangelicals such as Martin Lloyd-Jones, who argued that the church should stick to its time-honoured messages. These internal arguments probably left the wider public more confused about what Protestantism actually stood for. At the same time, Pope Paul VI's 1968 encyclical *Humanae Vitae* restated the Catholic Church's view that all forms of artificial contraception were 'intrinsically wrong', thereby alienating many who were hoping for a more pragmatic position. The gaps between church teaching and the reality of people's lives seemed to be growing dangerously wide. For the historian Callum Brown, indeed, the period from 1963 saw nothing less than the 'death of Christian Britain'. As a result of the social and cultural changes of these years, he writes, 'the generation that grew up in the sixties was more dissimilar to the generation of its parents than in any previous century'.[5] Church membership is notoriously difficult to measure, but on all the main indices – regular attendance at services, the number of baptisms and confirmations, marriage ceremonies conducted in churches – there were substantial declines in the 1960s and 1970s. Many people retained a private and often fairly vague belief in God, and generally accepted most of the main tenets of Christian morality beyond teaching on sexual behaviour, but interaction with the more organized elements of religious observance became less frequent. It became harder and harder even for established churches to claim that they truly represented, or spoke for, the nation, and each new generation that grew up seemed more distant from the faith.

The most dynamic church communities were often those sustained by people who had brought their faith from outside the UK. Many immigrants from the Caribbean were committed Christians, but some were quickly alienated by the racism they experienced at local Church of England services and established their own congregations. Black Pentecostal churches – a branch of Protestantism that emphasizes the direct personal experience of God and the Holy Spirit – grew significantly in urban areas, particularly London and Birmingham. Immigration from Asia and Africa saw a substantial rise in the visibility of Muslim, Hindu, and Sikh faiths in the UK. In 1961, there were an estimated 50,000 Muslims in England and Wales, with 30,000 Hindus and 16,000 Sikhs. By the time of the 2011 census, these figures had increased to 2.7 million Muslims, 816,000 Hindus, and 423,000 Sikhs.[6] There was an associated transformation of the urban landscape with the construction of Islamic mosques, Hindu temples, Sikh gurdwaras, and Buddhist shrines. There were only nine mosques in 1960, but 200 by 1986.[7] Schools, workplaces, and community spaces around the UK were transformed by new religious practices, symbols, and sensibilities.

With the weakening hold of the Protestant churches, and the growth of other religious communities, it no longer made sense to describe the UK as a Christian nation. It was a multi-faith, pluralistic society, with many people not holding any strong religious beliefs at all. Legislation increasingly protected the rights of non-Christian religious observance – in 1976, Sikh motorbike riders were given an exemption from the law requiring the wearing of helmets – and religious education in schools diversified, with the government's updated guidance in 2010 asking that children learn about five world religions. The 1994 Sunday Trading Act, which relaxed (but did not abolish) restrictions on retailers operating on Sundays, was a recognition that it was not appropriate to preserve the day for Christian observance. This transition was by no means straightforward or without tension. Many non-Christians faced mockery or hostility as a result of their faith. The rise of secularism and pluralism also encouraged a response in most faiths, including Christianity, in the form of the growing prominence of fundamentalist interpretations and a return to original scriptures. In the wake of the 9/11 attacks in the United States by the radical Islamist group Al-Qaeda, and the subsequent US–UK interventions in Afghanistan and Iraq (see Chapter 1), there were significant tensions around the place of Muslims in UK society. A small number, usually young men, were attracted to teachings that emphasized the rapacity and duplicity of the West, and encouraged violent retribution. In July 2005, four suicide bombers carried out attacks in London which killed fifty-two people. Over the subsequent years, there were a series of violent incidents involving people inspired by radical Islamism, including the bombing of Manchester Arena in May 2017 which left twenty-three people dead. There was an associated expansion of security service surveillance of these groups, as well as wider civil society efforts to prevent radicalization and encourage the better integration of Muslim communities into UK society.

By the early twenty-first century, religious observance was far more of a personal choice than it had been 100 years earlier. There was much less family and social pressure to adhere to a faith, at least in most communities. The UK had one of the lowest rates of active religious practice in the world. Individuals could select from a wide variety of faith options, with information about them easily accessible from school age upwards, or they could explore their spirituality through a variety of other mystical, pagan, or astrology-based creeds. Alternatively, as we will see, they could seek to satisfy their needs through consumption.

## *Consumerism, Class, and Social Mobility*

In 1945, only around a third of households lived in homes that they owned. More than one in ten still did not have electricity, and over one in four either used an outdoor toilet or shared an indoor one. Around four in ten did not have a fixed bath – most took one bath a week, and deodorant use was limited. Although most households had a radio, televisions were still essentially unknown outside a small number of technology enthusiasts. Telephones were a little more common, but still unusual. Fewer than one in six owned a car, and for the majority of people mobility revolved around walking, bicycles, and public transport. Food shopping was mostly local, at a proliferation of bakers, butchers, and greengrocers, and because refrigerators were extremely rare, fresh produce could not be stored for any length of time. Much clothing was home-made. For most people, holidays involved short trips within the UK, perhaps to a seaside resort such as Blackpool or Llandudno – overseas excursions were rare, and aeroplanes were largely associated with military use. Young people, when they left school, went into low-paid jobs, and often had to contribute to family finances: there was insufficient economic potential to sustain a significant youth culture. Eating out was very much for special occasions. Entertainment revolved around the pub, cinema, local sports venues, and music and dance halls. Religious injunctions to restraint and self-control resonated in a society in which excess and personal gratification were generally difficult to achieve, at least on any regular basis. Class differences remained visible in workplaces and public spaces. Non-manual employment, an educated accent, and the ownership of cars and consumer durables could all mark people apart from the 'ordinary'.

Over subsequent decades, economic change generated a revolution in lifestyles, working patterns, and individual expectations. The UK became a consumer society with unprecedented levels of personal wealth and where class was more fluid and articulated in very different ways. From the mid-1950s, the end of rationing, high and relatively stable levels of employment, and significant increases in real wages led to a new, and much remarked upon, affluence. By the early 1970s, products that once defined status were now within reach of ordinary working people. More than half of households now lived in their own homes, owned a car, a fridge, and a vacuum cleaner. Almost all households possessed a television; over a third also had a telephone. Retailing had been transformed by the rise of the supermarket, of which there were around 5,000 in 1972. The arrival of the credit card (Barclaycard launched in 1966) started to give consumers much greater access to credit. As the disposable income of young people increased, the popular music and fashion industries expanded rapidly, and bands such as the Beatles and the Rolling Stones demonstrated the potential market not only for records but also for concert tickets and memorabilia. The restaurant industry grew, while by 1971 some 8 million Britons were holidaying overseas. At the same time, the establishment of the NHS, the expansion of local government and the education sector, and the growth of electrical and technical industries created a significant rise in the demand for professional and managerial roles. There were greater opportunities to obtain middle-class jobs and lifestyles, not so much because the UK was becoming fairer and enabling greater social mobility, but rather because the economy was changing structure. To contemporaries, though, it was easy to assume that the UK was witnessing the emergence of a 'classless' society.

The economic dislocations of the 1970s, and the return of mass unemployment, shattered the complacent belief that affluence could be shared by all. Inequalities between the rich and poor grew, and gaps between north and south became increasingly apparent. Nevertheless, average incomes and consumer spending continued to rise and more and more consumer appliances and durables came within reach of ordinary households. Microwaves, freezers, dishwashers, video recorders, personal computers, and CD players became widespread by the 1980s, while later decades saw the rise of the mobile phone, MP3 music player, and tablet. Home ownership peaked in 2006 at 71% of households; DIY and home improvement underwent a related boom. The proportion of household spending on food declined significantly, despite a shift to more varied and expensive products. Eating out, takeaways, and home deliveries also became more common. Clothing became far cheaper with the arrival of low-cost manufacturing from Asia. The opening of the Channel Tunnel and the emergence of low-cost airlines in the mid-1990s made international travel even more accessible, especially to young people. Items and experiences previously regarded as luxuries were now becoming necessities.

The rise of the consumer society did not just involve accumulating more things, it also altered how individuals interacted with the world and how they defined themselves. Cars made people more mobile and turned remote places into accessible ones. City environments were remodelled to cater for cars, motorways were laid across the country, and out-of-town shopping centres lured consumers into new citadels of consumption. Telephones and computers provided new ways of connecting with people both local and distant. More fundamentally, consumption became more central to individual identity. Advertisers bombarded individuals with hundreds of invitations to buy every day. As Raymond Williams recognized in 1960, advertisers appealed to our fantasies and desires with a 'highly organised and professional system of magical inducements and satisfactions': 'You do not only buy an object: you buy social respect, discrimination, health, beauty, success, power to control your environment.'[8] This is not to say that individuals were passively duped by simplistic retail slogans; rather it is a recognition of the immense cumulative power of the underlying ideals of consumerism conveyed in the millions of advertising communications that everyone was exposed to: namely, that buying something will make us a little bit happier, that a new outfit will make us more confident, that an upgraded mobile phone will make us more productive. The offering of personal loans and credit agreements brought products into reach even for people without the resources at hand. The internet took further the historic promise of the mail-order catalogue that meaningful consumption could happen within the home; thousands of pounds could now be spent with a few clicks of a button. More creatively, the extended consumer landscape provided new opportunities for people to come together around particular interests and subcultures. Many came to define themselves around the consumer and leisure interests rather than their work, religion, or background. Indeed, 'going shopping' became a leisure activity in its own right, undertaken by millions every week.

From the 1980s, the increasing belief in the creativity of the market, as opposed to state planning and public ownership, brought consumerist language and principles into new areas of life. Providers of health, education, and other services were expected to offer choice, to guarantee minimum standards of delivery, and to address the public as consumers rather than as citizens. Schools were ranked in league tables according to learning outcomes so that parents could exercise their market judgement and shun poor providers. University students were required to pay fees for their degree programmes, and asked at the end about their levels of 'satisfaction'. Competition in providing such satisfaction was supposed to drive improvement across the sector. Individuals were invited to make choices and navigate their own paths in almost all areas of life – options which could be empowering, but also had the potential to be overwhelming, especially for those without the right information or expertise to make judgements.

Margaret Thatcher's market-based conservatism sought to create a more open and meritocratic society where everyone could participate in the fruits of consumerism – a 'property-owning democracy'. On the face of it, the UK's entrenched class structures did become more fluid. The further decline of industrial and manufacturing work from the 1980s, and the rise of retail, service, and IT-related employment, eroded the often stark divide between manual and non-manual work that characterized the UK in the first half of the twentieth century. As many traditionalist media commentators lamented, it became harder and harder to make social distinctions by observing an individual's attire or possessions, given that cars, watches, mobile phones, and branded fashions had become so widely available. The expansion of higher education also broke down some of the barriers limiting access to professional and managerial work. In 1954, little more than 3% of 18- to 21-year-olds went to university. By 1980, this had risen to 17%, and in 2019, twenty years after Tony Blair set a target of 50% of young adults participating in higher education, this symbolic threshold was reached. The following year, a record 23.3% of 18-year-olds from low-participation neighbourhoods were accepted onto a full-time university degree programme.

While these developments were undoubtedly impressive, however, they did not tell the whole story. In reality, underlying social mobility was limited by international standards. Social inequalities increased in the 1980s and 1990s, and then rose again in the decade of austerity after 2010. There were differences in life expectancy of as much as ten years between different parts of the UK. An individual's background continued to have a strong influence on their likelihood of going to a top-ranked university or obtaining a leading role in politics, the media, or the legal system. The credentialism encouraged by wider higher education and training gave valuable opportunities to graduates, but left the 50% of non-graduates in an increasingly difficult position, especially as skilled manual work declined. It was no coincidence that educational background became one of the key predictors of political affiliation, with many non-graduates unconvinced about whether the modern globalized economy, and particularly the mobility of labour, worked in their favour. The consumer society offered glittering material riches and the appearance of equal opportunities, but for many people the rewards remained illusory or out of reach.

## *Media and Popular Culture*

In most histories of the UK, the media tend to remain in the background, featuring perhaps in discussions of political communication or the rise of entertainment industries. In terms of how individuals in the UK actually spent their time, however, there is a good case for suggesting that the rise of media consumption from the Second World War to the first decades of the twenty-first century was the biggest single change in the everyday lives of ordinary people. The UK has always been a media nation. From the second half of the nineteenth century, its consumption of newspapers, magazines, and books matched or exceeded comparable countries around the world, and there was a swift and eager uptake of each of the new media forms of cinema, radio, and television. By the 2020s, UK adults were regularly spending more time using different forms of media than sleeping or working. A huge proportion of our lives are spent online – indeed, in a world of smartphones, smart watches, sleep-tracking devices, and internet-enabled domestic appliances, it is increasingly difficult to make meaningful distinctions between online and offline worlds. Individuals could access more information, and had greater choice over precisely what they consumed, than ever before. The national mass culture of the twentieth century gave way to a global and individualized media landscape in the twenty-first century.

We can identify three distinct periods of media usage in the decades after 1945. Until the mid-1950s, the UK's media culture was still dominated by newspapers, radio, and cinema. The UK had an unusually nationalized and competitive newspaper market, which reached its peak in the early 1950s, when some 85% of adults saw a paper every day. There was a sharp distinction in tone and content between newspapers serving the political and social elites, such as *The Times* and the *(Manchester) Guardian*, and those aimed at a more popular audience, such as the *Daily Mirror* and the *Daily Express* (both selling more than 4 million copies a day). The Sunday papers were even more successful, with the racy *News of the World* selling an astonishing 8.4 million copies per issue in 1951; given each paper was read by around three people, this meant that it was seen by half of all UK adults most weeks. Since the 1920s, the press had been forced to compete with radio in the delivery of news. The BBC was established in 1922 as the British Broadcasting *Company*, becoming a Corporation by royal charter in 1927, and had a monopoly over the airwaves. Because it was funded by a licence fee, and did not have to compete with other stations, it was able to develop a powerful ethos of public service broadcasting, which was understood to mean impartiality, the avoidance of controversy, support for the established churches, and the maintenance of (middle-class) standards of propriety and respectability. Two-thirds of households owned a radio set by the end of the 1930s, but this increased with the demand for war news and the introduction of cheaper 'utility' sets. By 1944, over 16 million people were tuning in to the BBC's 9 p.m. news programme. After the war, the BBC's output was restructured into three services, aimed at different sections of what was perceived to be the 'cultural pyramid': a Light Programme, with variety and popular music; the Home Service, offering a mixture of news, features, and music; and a Third Programme, focused on classical music and documentaries on high culture.

Outside the home, the cinema was the main media form. Cinema-going peaked in 1946 with

1,635 attendances across the year – the equivalent of a third of the population going once a week. The film habit was evident across the social spectrum, but, in contrast to other formats, younger working-class people were the highest attendees, and women went more than men. Hollywood-produced escapist entertainment was the main fare, although by the 1940s the UK-based industry was also responsible for some major successes, including Alfred Hitchcock's thrillers, Ealing Studio's comedies, and patriotic war films. In many respects, the press, radio, and film complemented each other well. The press was politically partisan, inquisitive, and, at times, irreverent; the BBC was balanced, respectable, and dependable; the cinema provided celebrity-fuelled glamour and entertainment. Together, the three helped to create a national 'imagined community' involving a shared news agenda, a predictable series of annual events – from the FA Cup football final and Wimbledon tennis to the Last Night of the Proms and Armistice Day – and a recognizable constellation of stars, celebrities, and other public figures, including the royal family, politicians, entertainers, and authors.

From the mid-1950s, this balance was increasingly disturbed by the rise of television. The BBC had launched a television service from London's Alexandra Palace in November 1936, and filmed George VI's coronation the following year. Only a couple of hours of material were broadcast per day, however, the signals did not yet travel across the whole country, and television sets remained expensive and experimental. The service was suspended in 1939 with the onset of the Second World War and did not resume until 1946. Two events transformed television's fortunes in the 1950s. The first was the coronation of Queen Elizabeth II in June 1953. The intense public interest in the ceremony led to many either buying a set or crowding into the homes of those who already owned one. The BBC's heavy investment in filming the proceedings produced a compelling spectacle. The audience was an unprecedented 22 million, the first time that a television audience had exceeded the radio one. Television's momentum was reinforced in 1955 by the introduction of a second channel, Independent Television (ITV), this time funded by advertising. The breaking of the BBC's monopoly was hugely controversial, and generated fears that culture would be coarsened by the materialism of the commercial breaks and the populism of shows seeking to appeal to the widest possible audiences. ITV was certainly widely watched, and forced the BBC to shake up its own output, but it was still fairly carefully regulated, and remained committed to addressing a respectable, mainstream, family audience. The BBC, granted a second channel in 1964, and ITV dominated the television landscape throughout the 1960s and 1970s.

Television was immensely popular, and as a result became immensely powerful. 'The box' was the most sought-after consumer item of the 1950s. In 1954, boosted by the coronation, around 3.25 million households owned a television licence; this figure doubled by 1957, and virtually doubled again by 1965. By 1969, over 90% of UK households had a television, and many were upgrading to bigger sets broadcasting in colour. Audiences were absorbed. By 1961, a survey found that the average UK adult spent thirteen and a half hours a week watching television, almost two hours a day. Twenty years later, this had risen to eighteen hours a week, nearly three hours a day, at a time when there was no early morning or late night broadcasting. Television quickly became people's main source of information about the world, and politics, sport, and entertainment all had to adapt to its demands. During the 1960s, it became the central arena of politics, with election campaigns, news releases, and interviews all structured around the opportunities provided by the main televised news programmes and current affairs shows. Ambitious politicians needed to be telegenic to be successful, and to adjust their language to the 'soundbites' required for the camera. The popular music industry and leading sports associations altered their practices for broadcasters to showcase their output, and were able to reach whole new audiences as a result. Celebrity culture was powerfully reinforced, as was consumerism, with advertisers relishing a potent new way of entering the home. Cinema and radio were hard-hit: the former lost a considerable share of its audience and the latter increasingly served as a background medium. Newspapers responded either by providing more detailed and analytical reporting than was available on television, or by providing the brash, intrusive, and sexualized content that television was not yet able to provide.

Until the 1980s, television reinforced the national culture that had emerged in mid-century. BBC and ITV held a captive television audience between three channels, and although there were nods to youth subcultures and minority interests, the bulk of programming was aimed at a mainstream audience. Peak-time shows regularly reached huge audiences of 10 and even 20 million viewers. Channel 4 (in Wales, the Welsh-language S4C) was launched in 1982 with the explicit instruction of innovating for the variety of tastes in an increasingly pluralistic society, and there were new strands of programming for different ethnic audiences (*Black on Black*, *Eastern Eye*) and sexualities (*Out on Tuesday*). It was only from the 1990s, though, that the media environment moved decisively into a new, more stratified and globalized era. The television landscape altered significantly with deregulation and the emergence of new satellite, cable, digital, and then online broadcasting platforms. The three- or four-channel, nationally focused landscape was radically transformed by the emergence of literally hundreds of channels, many transmitting from locations around the world, and catering for almost every possible interest. With time-shifting and on-demand capability, individuals could choose their own schedules, rather than being confined to those provided by the leading broadcasters. The BBC and ITV saw their audiences gradually shrink and fragment, and were forced to split their own provision across various channels.

At the same time, the rise of the internet fundamentally changed the media landscape. The first website was launched in August 1991 by the UK computer scientist Tim Berners-Lee, and in April 1993 the software underpinning the World Wide Web was put into the public domain. Over the next few years, numerous companies and entrepreneurs explored the potential of the internet as a way of presenting, storing, and searching information, connecting people, selling products, and creating new virtual worlds. Existing media providers started developing an online presence, with the BBC and *Daily Telegraph* being early adopters in 1994. Google launched its search engine to the public in 1998 and gradually developed into the dominant structure organizing people's interaction with the internet, eventually monetizing this position by selling information about online activity to advertisers. In the early years of the twenty-first century, as network speeds improved and internet-enabled smartphones became widely used, online interaction and the uploading of user-generated content became central areas of activity. Facebook was launched to the public in 2006 and became the world's pre-eminent social networking site. Twitter emerged the following year as an accessible means of sharing short posts of text and images, and in 2010 Instagram demonstrated the potential of photo-sharing. Other media forms increasingly migrated online: newspapers were redesigned to appear on tablets and smartphones; television and radio channels were streamed through apps; and companies such as Netflix and Amazon started taking on the roles of film and television providers.

Even before the Covid-19 pandemic, the UK had become an online society. In 2018, for the first time, surveys found that UK adults spent more time on computers and smartphones than watching television (three hours eighteen minutes per day versus two hours fifty-nine minutes). In February 2020, 96% of households had internet access, and 76% were sufficiently confident to use it for sensitive activities such as online banking. The lockdowns and restrictions implemented to control the pandemic only accelerated these developments, with online video calls becoming a standard means of children interacting with teachers, office workers collaborating with colleagues, and friends and relatives maintaining their social connections. But the internet powerfully reinforced the tendency towards a more individualistic society. Other media forms had to deal with scarcity – limited space, limited pages, limited channels – and tended to focus on mainstream content that would generate large audiences. The internet had no such limitations, and could offer unprecedented degrees of choice, personalization, and self-curation, providing material at no or low cost in return for targeted advertising opportunities. It was also truly global: the national boundaries erected around publishing and broadcasting simply fell away. This allowed people to explore a wider range of ideas and cultural opportunities than ever before, and to connect more freely across the world, but it also lessened shared interactions with local and national communities. It was much easier to consume only certain types of content and to exclude others, existing in a cultural space not with neighbours and fellow national citizens, but with individuals dispersed around the world.

UK citizens live in a very different social environment in the 2020s than they did in the 1940s. In the more pluralistic, affluent, and culturally fragmented world of the twenty-first century, it is no longer possible, or indeed acceptable, to make the sorts of generalizations about swathes of society that would have been commonplace in earlier decades. In the 1940s, governments, businesses, and media producers made plans on the assumption that social groups were relatively predictable and that they would respect the expertise of those in power. Visions of the future could be centrally produced. Eight decades later, politicians and policy-makers face a more diverse, more informed, and more demanding public who expect to express their voice and to be heard. Attachments to political parties are more superficial and easily broken, and voters are prepared to shift their allegiances if they do not like what they hear. In such circumstances, it is harder to hold the UK together. Perhaps it is easier for leaders in Scotland,

Wales, and Northern Ireland to construct persuasive and meaningful visions of the future for their own citizens than for politicians in London to find an appeal that will bring together the UK's diverse peoples. Only time will tell.

# Afterword

This book has explored the history of the UK through six different layers of experience, and has argued that this provides the best means of understanding the dynamics of a pluralistic and diverse society, and of teasing out the varied ways in which political power operates. If we focus on a major political issue, such as Brexit, we can identify the different layers and integrate them into our analysis. The UK's membership of the EU was obviously at heart a question about the nation's role in the world, and which international connections it most valued. It was also very much about economic policy: was the EU constraining the UK's growth and preventing it from realizing other trading opportunities across the globe? But we cannot appreciate the emotions invested in the debates, or explain how people voted, without bringing in the other layers too. Many people's Euroscepticism was powerfully motivated by perceptions about the extent to which immigration from Europe, based on the EU's fundamental principle of free movement, put pressure on the UK's welfare state and limited health, educational, and employment opportunities for UK citizens. It is equally clear that the nature of the discussions about Brexit varied significantly in England,

Wales, Scotland, and Northern Ireland: location emerged as one of the most important predictors of voting patterns. Attitudes to social movements and rights campaigns are also very relevant. Political science research has demonstrated that positions on a 'liberal–authoritarian' scale – defined by responses to questions such as 'Censorship is necessary to uphold moral values' and 'We should be tolerant of those who lead unconventional lifestyles' – are becoming more powerful predictors of political behaviour than the traditional 'left–right' scale.[1] It is evident that the 'Remain' and 'Leave' camps tended to have different approaches to questions of race, gender, and sexuality, and some leading advocates of Brexit, including Nigel Farage and Boris Johnson, adopted a deliberately traditionalist and masculine patriotism in the campaigning. Frustration at the EU's enforcement of rights for immigrants and refugees was a notable area of contention. Finally, the referendum campaigning was very much oriented to our individualistic and mediated society. Information posted on Facebook and Twitter, and further disseminated in fragmented social media circuits, played a significant part in shaping the conversations that were happening across the UK.

That contemporary politicians have struggled to develop a persuasive vision of the future addressing these varied dynamics, and reflecting on the realities of the UK's position, was evident in the repeated, almost reflex, reference to the past during the Brexit debates – not just on the 'Leave' side, but also by 'Remain' campaigners, who often pointed to the benefits that had been achieved over recent decades, and then tended simply to warn about the dangers of leaving. This book has shown how much has changed since 1945, but it is hard not to think that the Hugh Thomas of 1959, quoted in the Introduction, would be bemused to find that sixty years after his scathing critique of the 'establishment', the UK elected an Etonian prime minister, steeped in Classics and the language of Churchill, sceptical of Europe, and full of the glories of Global Britain. Boris Johnson's bombastic rhetoric eventually proved to be no substitute for a coherent political programme, and with his downfall in the summer of 2022, the UK was still searching for a way of reconciling the forces pulling it in different directions.

# Further Reading

Histories of the UK are many and varied. Of the long-range histories that include substantial sections on the post-1945 period, I would recommend Callum Brown and Hamish Fraser, *Britain since 1707* (Harlow: Longman, 2010), James Vernon, *Modern Britain: 1750 to the Present* (Cambridge: Cambridge University Press, 2017), Peter Clarke, *Hope and Glory: Britain 1900–2000* (London: Penguin, 2004), David Edgerton, *The Rise and Fall of the British Nation: A Twentieth-Century History* (London: Allen Lane, 2018), Pat Thane, *Divided Kingdom: A History of Britain, 1900 to the Present* (Cambridge: Cambridge University Press, 2018), and Martin Pugh, *State and Society: A Social and Political History of Britain since 1870* (London: Bloomsbury, 2022). Of the volumes focusing on the post-1945 period, the most comprehensive and penetrating is Brian Harrison's two-part history *Seeking a Role? The United Kingdom 1951–1970* and *Finding a Role? The United Kingdom 1970–1990* (Oxford: Oxford University Press, 2009/2010). Other valuable overviews include Kenneth Morgan, *The People's Peace: British History since 1945* (Oxford: Oxford University Press, 2021), and Paul Addison, *No Turning Back: The Peaceful Revolutions of Post-War*

*Britain* (Oxford: Oxford University Press, 2010). Greater narrative detail, and an eye for everyday life, characterize the various works of David Kynaston (*Austerity Britain*, *Family Britain*, *Modernity Britain*, and *On the Cusp* [all London: Bloomsbury, 2010–21]) and Dominic Sandbrook (*Never Had It So Good: A History of Britain from Suez to the Beatles* [London: Little Brown, 2005] and subsequent volumes). There are also a range of thematic and multi-authored volumes such as Paul Addison and Harriet Jones (eds), *A Companion to Contemporary British History 1939–2000* (Oxford: Blackwell, 2005), and Francesca Carnevali and Julie-Marie Strange (eds), *Twentieth-Century Britain: Economic, Cultural and Social Change* (London: Routledge, 2007). On Scotland, see T.M. Devine, *The Scottish Nation: A Modern History* (London: Penguin, 2012); on Wales, John Davis, *A History of Wales* (London: Penguin, 2007); and on Northern Ireland, Marc Mulholland, *Northern Ireland: A Very Short Introduction* (Oxford: Oxford University Press, 2020). On the dynamics of the UK, see Linda Colley, *Acts of Union and Disunion* (London: Profile, 2014). For political facts and statistics, Roger Mortimore and Andrew Blick (eds), *Butler's British Political Facts* (London: Palgrave Macmillan, 2018) is unbeatable; equally good on social developments is A.H. Halsey with Josephine Webb, *Twentieth-Century British Social Trends* (London: Macmillan, 2000).

On specific themes addressed in this book, the following offer excellent starting points for further reading: on empire and foreign policy, John Darwin, *The Empire Project: The Rise and Fall of the British World-System* (Cambridge: Cambridge University Press, 2009), and Mark Garnett, Simon Mabon, and Robert Smith, *British Foreign Policy since 1945* (London: Routledge, 2018); on electoral trends, David Denver and Mark Garnett, *British General Elections since 1964: Diversity, Dealignment, and Disillusion* (Oxford University Press, 2021); on economic change, Jim Tomlinson, *Managing the Economy, Managing the People: Narratives of Economic Life in Britain from Beveridge to Brexit* (Oxford: Oxford University Press, 2017); on class, Selina Todd, *The People: The Rise and Fall of the Working Class, 1910–2010* (London: John Murray, 2014); on the welfare state, Nicholas Timmins, *The Five Giants: A Biography of the Welfare State*, 3rd edn (London: William Collins, 2017); on education, Peter Mandler, *The Crisis of the Meritocracy: Britain's Transition to Mass Education since the Second World War* (Oxford: Oxford University Press, 2020); on affluence, Avner Offer, *The Challenge of Affluence: Self-Control and Well-Being in the United States and Britain since 1950* (Oxford: Oxford University Press, 2006); on sex, gender, and the family, Claire Langhamer, *The English in Love: The Intimate Story of an Emotional Revolution* (Oxford: Oxford University Press, 2013), Jeffery Weeks, *The World We Have Won: The Remaking of Erotic and Intimate Life* (London: Routledge, 2007), and Helen McCarthy, *Double Lives: A History of Working Motherhood* (London: Bloomsbury, 2020); on race and immigration, see Paul Gilroy, *There Ain't No Black in the Union Jack: The Cultural Politics of Race and Nation* (London: Routledge, 2002), David Dabydeen, John Gilmore, and Cecil Jones (eds), *The Oxford Companion to Black British History* (Oxford: Oxford University Press, 2007), and Ian Sanjay Patel, *We're Here Because You Were There: Immigration and the End of Empire* (London: Verso, 2021); on individualism, Jon Lawrence, *Me Me Me: The Search for Community in Post-War England* (Oxford: Oxford University Press, 2019); and on secularization, Callum Brown, *The Battle for Christian Britain: Sex, Humanists and Secularisation, 1945–1980* (Cambridge: Cambridge University Press, 2019).

# Notes

### Introduction

1 Hugh Thomas, 'The Establishment and Society', in Hugh Thomas (ed.), *The Establishment: A Symposium* (London: Anthony Blond, 1959), pp. 14–20.
2 https://www.nationalarchives.gov.uk/slavery/pdf/britain-and-the-trade.pdf.

### Chapter 1 Seeking a Role

1 Winston Churchill, VE Day speech, 8 May 1945, reprinted in Winston S. Churchill, *Never Give In! Winston Churchill's Speeches* (London: Bloomsbury, 2013), p. 325.
2 Winston Churchill to Conservative Party meeting, Llandudno, 9 October 1948, in Churchill, *Never Give In!*, p. 374.
3 *Daily Express*, 4 October 1952, p.1.
4 Peter Hennessy, *The Secret State: Whitehall and the Cold War* (London: Penguin, 2002), p. 44.
5 David Edgerton, *Warfare State: Britain 1920–1970* (Cambridge: Cambridge University Press, 2005).
6 David Edgerton, *The Rise and Fall of the British Nation: A Twentieth-Century History* (London: Allen Lane, 2018), p. 75.
7 John Darwin, *The Empire Project: The Rise and Fall of the British World-System* (Cambridge: Cambridge University Press, 2009), p. 590.
8 Quoted in Dominic Sandbrook, *Never Had It So Good: A History of Britain from Suez to the Beatles* (London: Little Brown, 2005), p. 92.
9 Ross Christie, '"Britain's Crisis of Confidence": How Whitehall Planned Britain's Retreat from the extra-European World, 1959–68' (University of Stirling PhD thesis, 2004), p. 102.

10 Macmillan speech to the South African House of Parliament, 3 February 1960, available at https://www.speech.almeida.co.uk/harold-macmillan.
11 *Guardian*, 6 December 1962, available at https://www.theguardian.com/century/1960-1969/Story/0,,105633,00.html.
12 Hugh Gaitskell to Labour Party conference, 3 October 1962, available at https://www.cvce.eu/en/obj/speech_by_hugh_gaitskell_against_uk_membership_of_the_common_market_3_october_1962-en-05f2996b-000b-4576-8b42-8069033a16f9.html.
13 Margaret Thatcher Foundation archive, Speech to Conservative Rally at Cheltenham, July 1982, https://www.margaretthatcher.org/document/104989.
14 Margaret Thatcher Foundation archive, Speech to the College of Europe, September 1988, https://www.margaretthatcher.org/document/107332.
15 Nigel Farage, cited in Harry Lambert, 'The Strange Death of Labour Britain', *New Statesman*, 3–9 September 2021, p. 28.
16 Danny Dorling and Sally Tomlinson, *Rule Britannia: Brexit and the End of Empire* (London: Biteback Publishing, 2019), p. 28.

## Chapter 2  The Pursuit of Economic Growth

1 Labour Party, 'Let us Face the Future: A Declaration of Labour Policy for the Consideration of the Nation', in F.W.S. Craig (ed.), *British General Election Manifestos 1900–1974* (London: Macmillan, 1975), pp. 123–31.
2 Clement Attlee, 'A Message from the Prime Minister', 1 January 1947, available at https://www.nationalarchives.gov.uk/education/resources/attlees-britain/nationalisation-coal/.
3 Edgerton, *The Rise and Fall*.
4 Harold Macmillan, speech at Bedford, 20 July 1957, in Andrew Burnet (ed.), *Chambers Book of Speeches* (Edinburgh: Chambers, 2006), p. 608.
5 Sandbrook, *Never Had It So Good*, p. 80.
6 Harold Wilson, TV address, 19 November 1967, available at

https://commonslibrary.parliament.uk/pound-in-your-pocket-devaluation-50-years-on/.
7 https://commonslibrary.parliament.uk/pound-in-your-pocket-devaluation-50-years-on/.
8 Edgerton, *The Rise and Fall*, p. 347.
9 Chris Cook and John Stevenson, *Britain since 1945* (Longman: Harlow, 1996), p. 167.
10 James Callaghan, speech to Labour Party conference, 28 September 1976, available at http://www.britishpoliticalspeech.org/speech-archive.htm?speech=174.
11 Andrew Hindmoor, *Twelve Days That Made Modern Britain* (Oxford: Oxford University Press, 2019), pp. 26–7.
12 Edgerton, *The Rise and Fall*, p. 297.
13 Raphael Samuel, 'Mrs Thatcher and Victorian Values', in *Theatres of Memory, Volume II. Island Stories: Unravelling Britain* (London: Verso, 1998), p. 332.
14 Pat Thane, *Divided Kingdom: A History of Britain, 1900 to the Present* (Cambridge: Cambridge University Press, 2018), p. 352.
15 Cook and Stevenson, *Britain since 1945*, p. 169.
16 Tony Blair speech to Labour Party conference, 26 September 2005, available at https://www.theguardian.com/uk/2005/sep/27/labourconference.speeches.
17 Hindmoor, *Twelve Days*, p. 225.

## Chapter 3 From Cradle to Grave

1 William Beveridge, *Social Insurance and Allied Services* (London: HMSO, 1942), p. 6.
2 https://blog.nationalarchives.gov.uk/beveridge-report-foundations-welfare-state/.
3 Beveridge, *Social Insurance*, p. 6.
4 *Daily Mirror*, 2 December 1942, p. 1.
5 Jim Tomlinson, *Democratic Socialism and Economic Policy: The Atlee Years, 1945–1951* (Cambridge: Cambridge University Press, 2002), p. 261.
6 Thane, *Divided Kingdom*, p. 198.
7 Aneurin Bevan speech at Manchester, 4 July 1948,

available at https://www.sochealth.co.uk/national-health-service/the-sma-and-the-foundation-of-the-national-health-service-dr-leslie-hilliard-1980/aneurin-bevan-and-the-foundation-of-the-nhs/bevans-speech-to-the-manchester-labour-rally-4-july-1948/.

8. Martin Chick, *Changing Times: Economics, Policies, and Resource Allocation in Britain since 1951* (Oxford: Oxford University Press, 2020), p. 194.
9. Roger Mortimore and Andrew Blick (eds), *Butler's British Political Facts* (London: Palgrave Macmillan, 2018), p. 491.
10. *Daily Mirror*, 3 September 1958.
11. Matthew Young, 'Racism, Tolerance and Identity: Responses to Black and Asian Migration into Britain in the National and Local Press, 1948–72' (University of Liverpool PhD thesis, 2012), pp. 167, 197–8.
12. *Daily Express*, 12 October 1966, p. 10.
13. Enoch Powell, 'Birmingham Speech', in Bill Smithies and Peter Fiddick (eds), *Enoch Powell on Immigration* (London: Sphere Books, 1969), pp. 40–1.
14. Brett Bebber, '"We Were Just Unwanted": Bussing, Migrant Dispersal, and South Asians in London', *Journal of Social History*, 48/3 (2015), pp. 635–61.
15. Brian Abel-Smith and Peter Townsend, *The Poor and the Poorest* (London: Bell, 1965), pp. 19, 62–3.
16. Kate Pickett and Richard Wilkinson, *The Spirit Level: Why More Equal Societies Almost Always Do Better* (London: Allen Lane, 2009).
17. Thane, *Divided Kingdom*, p. 322.
18. Norman Tebbit, speech to the Conservative Party conference, 15 October 1981, quoted in Anthony Jay (ed.), *Lend Me Your Ears: Oxford Dictionary of Political Quotations*, 4th edn (Oxford: Oxford University Press, 2010), p. 307.
19. Margaret Thatcher, *Women's Own*, 31 October 1987, available at https://www.margaretthatcher.org/document/106689.
20. Peter Lilley speech to the Conservative Party conference, 7 October 1992, available at https://www.totalpolitics.com/articles/news/peter-lilley-stands-down%E2%80%A6-and-green-campaigners-say-he-wont-be-missed.

21 Thane, *Divided Kingdom*, p. 379.
22 Nicholas Timmins, *The Five Giants: A Biography of the Welfare State*, 3rd edn (London: William Collins, 2017), p. 4.
23 Thane, *Divided Kingdom*, p. 366.
24 Charles Moore, *Margaret Thatcher, Herself Alone* (London: Penguin, 2019), p. 79.
25 Theresa May speech to the Conservative Party conference, 7 October 2002, available at https://www.theguardian.com/politics/2002/oct/07/conservatives2002.conservatives1.
26 Tony Blair speech, Toynbee Hall, 18 March 1999, available at https://www.theguardian.com/politics/1999/mar/19/politicalnews.politics.
27 https://commonslibrary.parliament.uk/research-briefings/cbp-8585/.
28 https://www.health.org.uk/publications/reports/the-marmot-review-10-years-on.

## Chapter 4 A Disunited Kingdom?

1 'Better together' was the slogan of the 'No' campaign slogan in the 2014 referendum on Scottish independence.
2 John Oakland, *British Civilization: An Introduction*, 7th edn (London: Routledge, 2011), p. 27.
3 For 1951, see Mortimore and Blick (eds), *Butler's British Political Facts*, pp. 471–2. For 2019, see https://www.ons.gov.uk/peoplepopulationandcommunity/populationandmigration/populationestimates/articles/overviewoftheukpopulation/january2021.
4 *Guardian*, 14 April 1945, available at https://www.theguardian.com/politics/2020/apr/14/snp-wins-first-seat-in-westminster-robert-mcintyre-1945.
5 Graham Walker, 'Scotland, Northern Ireland, and Devolution, 1945–1979', *Journal of British Studies*, 49/1 (2010), pp. 117–42 (p. 119).
6 Stephen Howe, 'Questioning the (Bad) Question: "Was Ireland a Colony?"', *Irish Historical Studies*, 36/142 (2008), pp. 138–52.
7 Sir James Craig, Northern Ireland House of Commons,

24 April 1934, cited in Jonathon Bardon, *A History of Ulster* (Belfast: The Blackstaff Press, 1992), pp. 538–9.
8 https://www.irishnewsarchive.com/wp/irish-republican-army-ira-begins-the-campaign-of-resistance-to-british-occupation-11-december-1956.
9 Report of the Bloody Sunday Inquiry, available at https://www.gov.uk/government/publications/report-of-the-bloody-sunday-inquiry.
10 David Torrance, '"Taking the Border out of Politics" – the Northern Ireland Referendum of March 1973, 21 November 2019', available at https://constitution-unit.com/2019/11/21/taking-the-border-out-of-politics-the-northern-ireland-referendum-of-march-1973/.
11 Thane, *Divided Kingdom*, p. 428.
12 *Guardian*, 12 April 2021, available at https://www.theguardian.com/politics/2021/apr/12/union-in-peril-as-pm-speaks-for-england-alone-former-civil-servant-warns.

## Chapter 5  People Power

1 Betty Friedan, *The Feminine Mystique* (Harmondsworth: Pelican, 1982 [1963]), p. 9.
2 Sheila Rowbotham, *Promise of a Dream: Remembering the Sixties* (London: Penguin, 2001), p. 162.
3 Sheila Rowbotham, 'Women's Liberation and the New Politics', in Micheline Wandor (ed.), *Once a Feminist: Stories of a Generation* (London: Virago, 1990), pp. 11–13.
4 Women's Liberation Workshop Statement (1970) in Wandor (ed.), *Once a Feminist*, pp. 240–1.
5 Germaine Greer, *The Female Eunuch* (London: Paladin, 1972), p. 19.
6 Jon Lawrence, *Me Me Me: The Search for Community in Post-War England* (Oxford: Oxford University Press, 2019), p. 226.
7 https://www.ons.gov.uk/employmentandlabourmarket/peopleinwork/earningsandworkinghours/bulletins/genderpaygapintheuk/2020.
8 Lord Arran, House of Lords Debates, 21 July 1967, vol. 285, cc. 522–6.

9  Graham Hunt, *Oz*, January 1971, quoted in Jonathon Green, *All Dressed Up: The Sixties and the Counter-Culture* (London: Pimlico, 1999), p. 390.
10 Gay Liberation Front Manifesto, 1971, quoted in Breanne Fahs (ed.), *Burn It Down! Feminist Manifestos for the Revolution* (London: Verso, 2020), pp. 53–70.
11 The Macpherson Report, 1999, available at https://assets.publishing.service.gov.uk/government/uploads/system/uploads/attachment_data/file/277111/4262.pdf.
12 *Guardian*, 29 July 2020, available at https://www.theguardian.com/uk-news/2020/jul/29/george-floyd-death-fuelled-anti-racism-protests-britain.
13 Margaret Thatcher, speech to UN, 8 November 1989, available at https://www.margaretthatcher.org/document/107817.

## Chapter 6  Looking after Number 1

1 1944 Education Act, available at https://www.legislation.gov.uk/ukpga/Geo6/7-8/31/contents/enacted.
2 Cited in Jay (ed.), *Lend Me Your Ears*, p. 244.
3 Bryan Wilson, *Religion in a Secular Society* (Harmondsworth: Penguin, 1969), p. 14.
4 Report of the Committee on Homosexual Offences and Prostitution ['Wolfenden Report'] (London: HMSO, 1957), pp. 9–10.
5 Callum Brown, *The Death of Christian Britain: Understanding Secularisation 1800–2000* (London: Routledge, 2001), p. 54.
6 Mortimore and Blick (eds), *Butler's British Political Facts*, pp. 589, 585.
7 Callum Brown and W. Hamish Fraser, *Britain since 1707* (Harlow: Pearson, 2010), p. 593.
8 Raymond Williams, 'The Magic System', *New Left Review*, I/4 (July–August 1960), pp. 27–32 (pp. 27, 29).

### Afterword

1 Paula Surridge, 'Brexit and Public Opinion: The Left–Right Divide', 30 January 2019, available at https://ukandeu.ac.uk/the-left-right-divide/.

# Index

Abel-Smith, Brian 94–5
abortion 146
Acheson, Dean 33, 36, 48
Adams, Gerry 133
advertising 52, 143, 149, 184, 191, 192
Afghanistan 42–3, 44, 45, 179
agriculture 53, 116
AIDS 155–6
Algeria 30
Al-Qaeda 42, 179
Anglo-Irish Agreement (1985) 125
Anglo-Irish Treaty (1921) 13, 109
anti-colonialism 30, 158
anti-racism 139, 140, 157–63
Argentina 37
Arran, Lord (Arthur Gore, eighth Earl of Arran) 153
Astor, Nancy 142
atheism 172–3
Attlee, Clement 49
    economic policy 52–4
    NHS 86–8
    welfare policy 84–6, 88
Australia 10, 11, 41, 48

Bank of England 53, 74, 75, 77
Barbados 10, 32

Barclays Bank 3, 182
Beaumont Society 153
Belfast 69, 108, 119, 121, 123
Berners-Lee, Tim 194
Bevan, Aneurin 86, 87, 88, 97
Beveridge, William, 80–2, 84, 88, 90, 94, 96–7, 104, 107
    Beveridge Report (1942) 80–2, 84–6
Bevin, Ernest 24
'Big Bang' 73
Birmingham 69, 125, 178
Black Lives Matter 163
Black Power 161
Blair, Tony 75
    child poverty 105
    economic policy 75–7
    foreign policy 42–5
    globalization 76
    Good Friday Agreement (1998) 132–4
    Iraq war 43–4
    Scotland 130–2
    sex, regulation of 156–7
    Wales 130–2
    welfare policy 103–5
'Blitz' 14, 49
Blix, Hans 43
'Bloody Sunday' (1972) 124
Boateng, Paul 162

Bradlaugh, Charles 173
Bretton Woods agreement (1944) 62
Bristol 10
   bus boycott (1963) 159–60
   Colston statue toppled (2020) 163
British Broadcasting Corporation (BBC) 3, 113–14, 172, 189–91, 193–4
British Empire 4–5
   decolonization 6, 7, 32–3, 35–6, 58, 109, 121
   expansion of 10–11, 108
   'modernization' 25–6
   and Second World War 22
British Medical Association 86
British Telecom (BT) 72
Brixton Black Women's Group 148
Brooke, Basil 119–20
Brown, Gordon
   economic policy 75–7
   environmental policy 166
   welfare policy 103–5
Bruges speech (1988) 39
Burma 22
Bush, George W., 43

Callaghan, James
   economic policy 64–6
Cameron, David
   EU referendum (2016) 46–7
   financial crash 77–8
   foreign policy 44
   same-sex marriage 157
   welfare policy 83, 106–7
Campaign for Homosexual Equality (CHE) 155
Canada 11, 41
Canary Wharf 73
car manufacture 3, 58, 60, 144
car ownership 3, 56, 180, 181, 182, 183–4, 186
Cardiff 12, 111, 122
Catholicism 7, 9, 109, 111, 118–20, 123–5, 172, 177
Chamberlain, Neville 14
Channel 4 193
Channel Tunnel 40, 183
China 11, 25, 37, 76
Christianity 169, 171–80
Church of England 115, 172, 178
Churchill, Winston 5, 6, 152, 200
   appointed prime minister 14
   nuclear weapons 24
   speeches 17–18
cinema 188, 189–90, 192
City of London 4, 73, 130
class 47, 57, 86, 89–90, 130, 158, 180–7
Clean Air Act (1956) 164
climate change 51–2, 79, 140, 164–7
coal industry 12–13, 49, 50
   decline 61, 110
   industrial action 61, 63, 71, 130

Cold War 19, 25–6
  end of 40
Colonial People's Defence Association 158
Commonwealth 18, 19, 25, 33, 34, 36, 41, 48, 57
conscription 24, 32
Conservative Party
  'Black Wednesday' (1992) 74–5
  economic policy 54–5, 63, 67–74, 78–9
  environmental policy 166–7
  European policy 33–4, 39–40
  financial crash (2007–8) 77–8
  general elections 2, 57, 63, 70, 88, 130, 135, 168
  inter-war success 14
  'Nasty Party' 103–4
  Northern Ireland 124–5
  Scotland 117, 129–30, 135
  same-sex marriage 157
  sexual offences 152
  Wales 129–30
  welfare policy 83, 88–9, 98–102, 106–7
consumerism 56, 180–7, 192
Covid-19 pandemic 78–9, 83–4, 107, 137, 150, 195
Craig, James 119–20
Cyprus 11, 32

*Daily Express* 24, 92, 188
*Daily Mail* 37
*Daily Mirror* 41, 84, 91, 188
*Daily Telegraph* 194

de Gaulle, Charles 34
Delors, Jacques 39
Democratic Unionist Party 123
devaluation of sterling (1967) 58
Dublin 13, 125

East India Company 10
Easter Rising 13, 109, 118
Eden, Anthony 27–9
Edinburgh 111, 146, 167
education 89–90, 104–5, 131–2, 172, 179, 185
Egbuna, Obi 161
Egypt 26–8
empire *see* British Empire
England
  geography 112
  nationalism 112, 137
  north–south divide 49, 71, 74
  population 113
  relationship with UK 8–9, 110
  sport 41, 59
environmental movement 140, 163–7
Equal Pay Act (1970) 144, 150
equality legislation 149, 150, 157, 162
euro 40, 45
European Community/European Union
  formation of 30–1
  UK's applications to join 33–4

European Community/
    European Union (*cont.*)
    UK departure ('Brexit') 6,
        19–20, 46–7, 78, 136–7,
        198–200
    UK joins (1973) 6, 34–5
    UK referendum (1975)
        35–6, 39
    UK referendum (2016) 47,
        111, 135–6
    UK relationship with
        20–1, 30–1, 35–6, 39,
        45–7
European Exchange Rate
    Mechanism (ERM) 39,
    74–5
European Free Trade
    Association (EFTA) 31
Evans, Gwynfor 127
Everard, Sarah 150
Ewing, Winifred 127

Facebook 194, 199
Falkland Islands 33
Falklands War (1982) 37–8,
    70
Farage, Nigel 46, 199
feminism 139–40, 141–50
financial crash (2007–8) 46,
    76–7
First World War 11, 12–13,
    116, 141
FitzGerald, Garret 125
Floyd, George 162–3
food banks 106
Foster, Arlene 149
France 11, 27–8, 30, 39, 58,
    172

Friedan, Betty 143
Friedman, Milton 62, 67
Friends of the Earth 164

Gaitskell, Hugh 34, 160
Gay Liberation Front (GLF)
    153–5
*Gay News* 155
Germany 11, 14, 19, 25, 30,
    39, 41, 80
    economic comparisons 30,
        57, 59
Ghana 2, 32
Glasgow 12, 69, 117, 121,
    127, 129, 173
'Glorious Revolution'
    (1688–9) 7
Good Friday Agreement
    (1998) 111, 132–4,
    136–7
Google 194
Graham, Billy 173
Great Britain, formation of 9
Green Party 165–6
Greenpeace 164
Greer, Germaine 146–7
Griffiths, Peter 92
Gulf War (1990–1) 41

Hayek, Friedrich 62, 67
Healey, Denis 65
Heath, Edward 70
    economic policy 63–4
    European policy 34, 36
    Northern Ireland 124–5
    Scotland 128
Hinduism 172, 178
homelessness 95, 101

Homosexual Law Reform
    Society (HLRS) 152
Hong Kong 11, 33, 37
housing 53, 69, 88–9, 105,
    180, 182, 183
  and race 91–2
  'right to buy' 68, 99, 100
Howe, Geoffrey 39
Hussein, Saddam 43

immigration 5, 35–6, 45–6,
    76, 158–9
  'hostile environment' policy
    93
  legislation 160–1
  religion 178
  and welfare 91–2, 106,
    198
Independent Television (ITV)
    191, 193–4
India 10–11, 60, 76
  independence 18, 22–3, 25,
    29
Indian Workers' Association
    158
industrial action 61, 63, 66,
    70–1, 97, 144
industrialization 4, 11–13,
    51, 173
inequality 51, 74, 79, 84, 96,
    100, 105–7, 183, 186–7
inflation 61, 63–5, 68, 75, 97
Institute of Race Relations
    159
International Monetary Fund
    (IMF) 4, 65, 97
internet 41, 170, 184, 188,
    194–6

Iran 69
Iraq 11, 41, 179
  Iraq war (2003) 43–5
Ireland 7, 9, 34, 109
  creation of Irish Free State
    13, 109, 119
  famine (1840s) 118
  *see also* Northern Ireland;
    Republic of Ireland
Irish Republican Army (IRA)
    111, 120, 123
  Provisional IRA 123–4,
    125–6, 132–3, 134
iron industry 12–13, 49, 53,
    54, 110
Islam 172, 178–80
Israel 27, 28, 62

Jamaica 10, 32
Japan 14, 19, 21, 22
  economic comparisons 57,
    59
Jenkins, Roy 175
Johnson, Boris 6, 200
  'Brexit' 47–8, 136–7
  Covid-19 pandemic 107
  economic policy 78–9
  foreign policy 48
  Northern Ireland 136–7
Jones, Claudia 3, 158, 159
Joseph, Keith 67
Judaism 172, 174

Kenya 26, 32
Keynes, John Maynard 21,
    50
Korean War 25
Kosovo 42, 43

Labour Party
  Beveridge Report (1942) 82
  devolution 130–2, 136
  economic policy 50, 52–4, 55, 64–5, 75–7
  election manifesto (1945) 50, 52
  emergence of 14
  European policy 34
  financial crash (2007–8) 76–7
  general elections 63, 82, 130, 135, 168
  Good Friday Agreement (1998) 132–4
  Iraq war 43–4
  'New Labour' 42, 75, 103, 105, 130, 132
  NHS 86–8
  Northern Ireland 123, 132–4
  nuclear weapons 24
  religion 173
  Scotland 117, 130–2, 135
  sex, regulation of 156–7
  Wales 115, 127–8, 130–2
  welfare policy 84–6, 94–6, 103–5
Lawrence, Stephen 162
Lawson, Nigel 39, 83
League of Coloured Peoples 158
LGBTQ+ activism 139–40, 149–57
Liberal Democrats 35, 106, 131, 165
Libya 44
Lilley, Peter 100

Liverpool 10, 69, 127, 137, 158
Lloyd George, David 115
Lloyd-Jones, Martin 176
Lloyds Bank 77
London 47, 101
  activism 3, 43, 144, 155–6, 158, 161, 162
  bombings (July 2005) 44, 179
  capital 9, 51, 108, 113, 135
  economy 4, 73, 130
  pollution 164
  religion 173, 178
  'riots' 69, 159
Lucas, Caroline 165

Maastricht Treaty (1992) 40
Macmillan, Harold 2, 5
  affluence 56
  economic policy 54–5
  European policy 33
  Suez crisis 28–9
  'Winds of Change' speech (1960) 32
Macpherson, William 162
Major, John
  'Black Wednesday' 74–5
  European policy 40, 45
Malaya 26, 32
Manchester 12, 69, 137, 179
Marmot, Michael 106
'Marshall Aid' 21
Mau Mau 26
May, Theresa 78
  environmental policy 166
  'hostile environment' policy 93

'Nasty Party' speech
    103–4
McGregor, Ian 71
McGuinness, Martin 133–4
media 113, 114, 138, 143,
    170, 187–96
Mellors, Bob 153
Methodism 172, 173
military expenditure 25, 49,
    57
Mini 3
minimum wage 75–6, 104
Minorities Research Group
    153
mobile phone 183, 186,
    194–5
monarchy 7–8, 9, 134, 191
monetarism 62, 67–8
Moody, Harold 158
Mountbatten, Louis 126, 134
Mowlam, Mo 133

Nasser, Gamal Abdel 26–27
National Health Service (NHS)
    81, 83, 91, 102, 103, 182
  Covid-19 pandemic 107
  creation 86–8
  internal market 102
  investment 104
national service 24, 32
National Union of
    Mineworkers (NUM) 61
nationalization of industry 50
Neave, Airey 125
New Cross Fire (1981) 162
new towns 53
New Zealand 10
Newcastle 12

*News of the World* 189
newspapers 113, 188–90,
    192–3
9/11 attacks 42, 43, 179
North Atlantic Treaty
    Organization (NATO) 4,
    25, 42, 44
North Western Homosexual
    Law Reform Committee
    153, 155
Northern Ireland
  creation of 13, 119
  discrimination against
      Catholics 120, 122
  elections 119
  European referendum
      (2016) 47, 111, 136
  Good Friday Agreement
      (1998) 132–4, 136–7
  geography 112
  industry 49, 110, 121
  parliament 119, 124
  population 113, 118
  referendum (1973) 124–5
  relationship with UK
      118–19, 196–7
  religion 16, 118, 120, 172
  Sexual Offences Act 1982
      155
  'troubles' 121–6
Northern Ireland Civil Rights
    Association (NICRA) 122
Northern Rock 77
Notting Hill Carnival 3, 158
nuclear weapons 3, 23–4, 127

Obscene Publications Act
    (1959) 175

oil production 65–6, 74, 128
O'Neill, Terence 120, 122
Organization of Petroleum Exporting Countries (OPEC) 63
Organization of Women of Asian and African Descent 148
Osborne, George 78
  welfare policy 83
*Oz* 154

Paisley, Ian 122, 123, 134
Pakistan 18, 22–3
Palestine 11, 23
Penguin Books 175
pensions 85, 94, 98, 106
Pitman, Robert 92
Plaid Cymru 110–11, 115, 127–8
  devolved elections 131
  general elections 128, 129
Pompidou, Georges 34
poverty 85, 94–6, 104–5, 106–7
Powell, Enoch 92, 161
Presbyterianism 172
privatization 62, 72
Protestantism 5, 7, 9, 108, 172–3, 176–8
Public Morality Council (PMC) 174, 175

race
  civil rights (US) 121
  race relations 160–1
  racialized thought 5, 26, 36
  racism 41
  'riots' 159
  and welfare 91–3
  *see also* anti-colonialism; anti-racism
radio 180, 188, 189, 191, 192
rationing 49, 53, 54, 181
Reagan, Ronald 41
religious belief 169, 171–80
Republic of Ireland 13, 112, 133; *see also* Ireland
Rhodesia 33, 37
Robinson, John 176
Rowbotham, Sheila 144–5
Royal Bank of Scotland 77
Royal Ulster Constabulary (RUC) 120, 122–3
Runcie, Robert 38

S4C 193
Salmond, Alex 135
Sands, Bobby 126
Saudi Arabia 60
Scargill, Arthur 71
Scotland
  devolution 16, 128–9, 131–2, 134–5
  devolution referendums 128–9, 131
  European referendum (2016) 47, 111, 135–6
  general elections 130, 135
  geography 112
  Green Party 166
  independence campaigns 110–11, 117–18, 134–5
  industry 12, 49, 71, 110, 121
  language 116

nationalism 127–30
oil 128
parliament 111
population 113
relationship with UK 8–9, 116–18, 129–30, 196–7
religion 116, 172
Scottish Office 116
Sexual Offences Act 1980 155
Scottish National Party (SNP) 110–11, 116–17, 127–8, 166
   devolved elections 131, 134–5
   general elections 128, 129, 135
   independence campaigns 134–5
   North Sea Oil 128
Second World War 14, 17, 27, 41, 80, 91, 109, 115, 191
   financial impact 17, 21, 25, 49, 59
Section 28 (Local Government Act 1988) 156
secularization 173–4, 177, 179
Sexual Offences Act (1967) 153, 155
Sheffield 12, 69, 137
Shelter 95, 101
Sherman, Alfred 67
shipbuilding 12–13, 49, 61, 69, 110, 127
Sikhism 172, 178
Singapore 11, 22, 32, 60

Single European Act (1986) 39
Sinn Féin 13, 132–4
slave trade 10, 51, 157, 163
South Africa 11, 32
Soviet Union
   Cold War 19, 25
   nuclear weapons 4
   superpower 5
steel industry 12–13, 53, 54, 69, 110
Stern, Nicholas 166
Stonewall 156
Sturgeon, Nicola 149
Suez crisis 5, 26–9
Suicide Act (1961) 175
*Sun* 37
Sunak, Rishi 79
Sunningdale Agreement (1973) 125
Swansea 12, 69, 121, 129
Syria 44

Taliban 42, 44
Tebbit, Norman 99
television 180, 182, 188, 190–4
textile industry 12–13, 49, 61
Thatcher, Margaret 6
   economic policy 60, 66–74, 185
   environmental policy 165
   European policy 39
   foreign policy 36–9
   general elections 66, 70
   industrial relations 70–1
   Northern Ireland 125–6
   poll tax 130

Thatcher, Margaret (*cont.*)
  Scotland 129–30
  speeches 38, 70, 165
  Wales 129–30
  welfare policy 83, 98–102
Thomas, Hugh 1–3, 5, 6, 8, 200
Timothy, Nick 78
Townsend, Peter 94–5
trade unions 61, 63, 70–1
Treaty of Rome (1957) 31
Trimble, David 133
Trussell Trust 106
Twitter 194, 199

Ulster Defence Association (UDA) 124
Ulster Protestant Volunteers (UPV) 122
Ulster Unionist Party 119
Ulster Volunteer Force (UVF) 122
unemployment 56, 61–2, 64, 69, 74, 75–6, 77, 183
  'New Deal' 104
  unemployment benefit 83, 85, 94, 98
union with Ireland (1800) 9
union with Scotland (1707) 9
United Kingdom, formation of 8–9
United Kingdom Independence Party (UKIP) 45–6
United Nations 4, 27, 43, 165, 167
United States
  Afghanistan 42, 44
  civil rights campaign 121
  Cold War 19, 25
  economic policy 62
  feminism 143
  independence of 10
  Iraq War 43
  LGBTQ+ activism 154
  9/11 attacks 42, 179
  nuclear weapons 4, 24
  settlement of 10
  Suez crisis 27–8
  superpower 5
  UK's economic relationship with 21, 48
universities 89, 131–2, 150, 169, 185, 186–7

Vietnam war 144
voting reform 13–14, 141–2, 169

Wales
  assembly 111
  devolution 16, 128–9, 131–2
  devolution referendums 128–9, 131, 132
  general elections 130
  geography 112
  industry 12, 49, 71, 110, 121
  language 114, 126, 193
  nationalism 126–30
  population 113
  relationship with UK 8–9, 114–15, 196–7
  religion 114–15, 172
Walter, Aubrey 153

# INDEX

*West Indian Gazette* 158
Williams, Raymond 184
Wilson, Harold
   devaluation (1967) 58
   economic policy 55, 58
   European policy 34–5
   general elections 63
   Northern Ireland 123
   resignation 64
   Wales 127
   welfare policy 94–6

'Winter of Discontent' 66
Wolfenden, John 152–3
Wolfenden report (1957) 152, 174–5
Wollstonecraft, Mary 141
Women's Liberation movement 143–8
World Bank 4

Zimbabwe 37